Praise for: Born in a Barn
A Memoir by Mary VanderKooy Guldemond

Loved this relatable story of growing up in a large family and emigrating to a new country with all of the joy and heartache that experience brings with it. One of the better memoirs I have read in the last decade!

- Sally Mills

I loved this lively and intimate story and could not put the book down. Some sections made me laugh out loud, while others reduced me to tears. I highly recommend this book!

- Annemarie Vander Veen

This is a deeply moving immigration story. The Dutch have a total world population of 30 million people, only 16 million of whom live in the Netherlands. In the Dutch diaspora there are many stories like Mary Guldemond's, but not many of them have been told with such a high level of honesty and grace. Her writing is frank, but she never stoops to passing off the hardships in the form of blaming others. Immigration is a struggle; there is no doubt about it. A story as carefully and colorfully crafted as this one is a fine reminder that the long journey has its own rewards. A good selection for book groups, and a good individual read for a generation wondering about the experiences of those who have gone before.

- Mary Vandergoot, author of the *Maggie Barnes Trilogy*

A fascinating memoir of a transplanted immigrant girl. A well-narrated account of home and family life, the immigration experience, the joys and sorrows along the way, all interspersed with informative, interesting, and incisive reflections by the author. Among the best in its genre that I have read.

- Harry Van Dyke, Professor Emeritus in History, Redeemer University

BORN IN A BARN

A MEMOIR

Mary VanderKooy Guldemond

COPYRIGHT © 2022
by Mary VanderKooy Guldemond

All rights reserved. Neither this publication nor any part of this publication may be reproduced or transmitted in any form or by any means, electronic or mechanical, including photocopying, recording or any information storage and retrieval system, without permission in writing from the author.

Printed in Canada

ISBN: 978-1-7390540-0-7

To my dear children
and grandchildren

BORN IN A BARN

PROLOGUE   1

PART I

1. Born in a Barn   6
2. Precious Memories   19
3. My Mother's Life Story   32
4. My Father's Life Story   50
5. No Longer Little   68
6. Water, Everywhere!   77
7. Saying Good-bye   86

PART II

8. Uneasy Transitions   97
9. School in Canada   105
10. Everyone Pitching In   113
11. My Teenage Years   121
12. My Mother and I   132
13. Nightmare   139
14. Trudy Becomes Ill   145
15. More Babies   159
16. Dominee's Visit   167
17. Losing Our Sister   171
18. Funeral   178
19. Grief   184

PART III

20. Opening the Floodgates   191
21. My Parents' Later Years   197
22. Still Waters   205

My Family's Birth Order   211

Acknowledgements   213

PROLOGUE

I stood there, stunned. I had walked into the Burlington Art Centre one day in 2012, and happened upon an art exhibit entitled "IMMIGRANT." It was by Rosemary Sloot, a London, Ontario, artist born in 1952, shortly after her parents immigrated from The Netherlands. She grew up in Waterford, not far from where I grew up. Rosemary began this series of paintings after her mother's deathbed revelation. Her mother told two of her daughters that she had only one regret: she wished that she had never immigrated to Canada from the Netherlands. The experience had been too difficult and too much had been lost. Learning this so shocked and saddened Rosemary, that it prompted her to begin researching and exploring the multiple layers of the immigrant experience.

As I slowly took in Rosemary's evocative paintings layering text and image, they had a profound effect on me. Many were sad, also hauntingly beautiful, such as the soft-focus painting of a window in a white Insulbrick house, three young children looking out at the wintry, desolate scene, bare tree branches bending in the wind. The most powerful and moving painting in the collection was a large diptych called "The Burden of the Immigrant." The painting depicted two separate worlds: on the left was a snowy,

Canadian winter scene with foreground twigs of a snow-covered thistle leaning sharply towards the left, and on the right was a Dutch country lane flanked by bare, wintry willow trees veering off out of sight towards the right. In oversize cursive handwriting, Rosemary had written at the bottom of the painting: "The burden of the immigrant is forever to be pulled between two worlds." As I made my way through the art exhibit, I was pulled back to this painting again and again. Finally, I sat on the viewing bench and let myself fully absorb its message. Tears welled up from deep within me. A fine and accomplished artist, Rosemary has poignantly told the story of Canadian immigrants who straddle two cultures.

Photo: courtesy of Rosemary Sloot

I, too, am the daughter of Dutch immigrants. My parents also made a life-altering decision when they chose to uproot their family out of a familiar environment, into the unknown of a new and strange country. I was ten years old when we arrived in Canada. In the early years, my parents encountered financial insecurity, hardships, illness, and loss. In her art exhibit, Rosemary Sloot captured what immigration might have meant for our parents, and by extension, for us, their children. What was the impact of that momentous decision for my parents? Did they have regrets?

What was the impact of our immigration on us, their children? What was it on me? The effect of immigration was compounded by the fact that I am one of many children. My family was large, very large. My parents immigrated with ten children in 1955 and had three more in Canada. What was the impact on me of being one of so many children?

Human beings have a need to feel special and to be special. Every one of us who starts life loved by parents feels unique and special, until we learn that we are all special, meaning that no one is really special. The question of being special is particularly poignant in large families, where individual needs are often submerged by the needs of the group. In our family, too, we struggled for attention, for a special place. We might be seen, but we did not often feel noticed or heard. We were not sure that we'd be missed if we were absent or gone.

Interestingly, while being part of a large family can be detrimental to one's personal identity formation, it can also provide an anchor, an identity for each member. As a member of our large family, I could feel special. When asked to introduce myself, I'd readily answer with "I belong to the large VanderKooy family in Simcoe." Our large family status allowed us to feel somewhat entitled. We were given more boxes of donated clothing than any other immigrant family because their families were not as large. We took for granted that nearby Dutch neighbours would give us free rides to church, because, after all, our car could not hold all of us. Our group identity had its own benefits.

Trudy was the second oldest child in our family of thirteen children. A few years after we immigrated to Canada, she became ill with hepatitis. Five years later she succumbed to this illness and died. She was 23 years old.

Before she died, Trudy was just a member of our large family. When she died, she became special. It seemed that Trudy figured larger in death than in life for us. As a family we gained a new distinctiveness in the Simcoe area. Not only were we part of that big family, but now we also had a sister who had died tragically and beautifully.

I was 18 years old when Trudy died. Her story profoundly affected the latter years of my childhood. There were times that Trudy and I were bedridden at the same time during her lengthy illness. We connected in unique ways. I was not prepared for the shock of losing my sister, and grieving her loss has been an ongoing process for me. I write about her life story in detail in this memoir of my childhood in order to treasure her memory and to honour the special person that she was for me.

Immigration Family Photo – 1955

Back row, left to right: John (Jan), Catherine (Tini), Simon (Siem), Trudy (Truus) Front row: Mary (Mieke), Jack (Jaap), James (Koos) van der Kooij, Elizabeth (Beppie), Maria van der Kooij (Marie), Magdalena (Heleentje) on her lap, Corrie, Jim (Koos).

PART I

1. BORN IN A BARN

Except for the morning rush, I liked Sundays. These days were quieter, more peaceful in the house than weekdays. My father did no work in the fields or in the barn other than milking the cows and feeding the animals. Sunday was also a simpler and more restful day for my mother - no laundry, no house cleaning, no cheese-making, no maids or assistants, and no servicemen at the door. She peeled enough potatoes to fill a huge pot the night before so that after church it took less time to get hot lunch ready. Then on Sunday, while the potatoes and cabbage were cooking, she browned and simmered the round steak in the cast iron Dutch oven in a half pound of butter to ensure plenty of gravy, and voila, dinner was on the table in a jiffy. After that, my parents retired to their bedroom for a long nap.

I vividly remember a beautiful, Pentecost Sunday afternoon. I think I was six years old, and at that time I already had four sisters and three brothers. My parents and the little ones had gone for their nap and except for my oldest brother, Siem, the rest of us headed outside. Wearing our wooden shoes, Truus, Tini, Jan, Corrie, and I walked in single file along the dike behind our house. The weather had just turned warm, the sky was a beautiful blue, and the water in the canal beside us rippled gently. In the distance I noticed small white triangles drifting slowly on the horizon. Tini explained to me that those were sailboats on the small lake north of us. We noticed all the buttercups that had sprung up, dotting the green meadows in the polder land below us, and we headed down the dike towards them. I wandered away from the others, delighting in the beauty all around me, and I happily picked an armful of golden yellow buttercups, then added some tiny daisies and purple clover to my growing bouquet. I wandered further, then lay on my back in the soft green grass. I held the bouquet to my nose, then held it further away, admiring the shapes and array of colours. I squeezed my eyelids almost shut to see a different, more abstract pattern through my eyelashes. I remember the sun warming my nose and a soft breeze lightly touching my curly hair and tickling my face. My eyes wandered up to where soft, white fluffy clouds gently changed their shapes as they lazily moved along in the azure sky. I felt such peace and calm. In the distance I could hear the soft, receding voices of my sisters and brother. I wondered about heaven as I lay in that field.

The warmth, the scents, and the images of this beautiful spring day have stayed with me. In my sixties I was once asked to identify my "happy place." The image that came most readily to mind was a warm, sunny Pentecost afternoon in a green pasture blanketed with yellow buttercups, a blue sky and soft white clouds overhead.

The Lord is my shepherd,
I shall not want.
Psalm 23

MY LIFE BEGAN on March 8, 1945, in a picturesque old home which nestled alongside a big canal we called "*De Vliet.*" I was the fifth child for Koos and Marie van der Kooij. The first ten years of my life I was "Mieke," but my full name as stated on my birth announcement was "Maria Elizabeth van der Kooij." These years prior to our immigration in 1955 are in hazy focus for me, but they feel relatively calm, secure, stable, and mostly carefree.

I was born in the historic "boerderij" or farm at 5 Zuidbuurt in the town of Maasland, which is just west of Rotterdam, The Netherlands. Ours was a typical old boerderij (pronounced "boer-duh-rye"), so it included a large cow stable, a small horse stable, and an attached pig barn at one end, a large mid-section, and family living quarters at the other end, all under one long roof. The building we lived in was neither a house nor a barn, it was both. Because of my birth's unusual setting, people have heard me claim that I was born in a barn, and that nine of my twelve siblings were born in this same barn, as were my father and his twelve siblings.

I will continue to use the word "boerderij" instead of "farm" because the word encompasses my childhood experience so much better. The word "boerderij" refers to the main structure, but it can also refer to the whole operation, which included the outbuildings and the farmland. Our boerderij was built in 1711 and it was one of the oldest in the area. In the 1960's it was declared an historic monument and after that date, exterior alterations to the building were no longer permitted. Currently, the three-century-old boerderij is a well-developed, fascinating retreat and tourist destination named *De Karperhoeve* (see karperhoeve.nl).

I WILL IMAGINE for a moment that I am still 8 years old, and that I'm coming home from the town of Maasland on my bicycle. As I approach the long bridge spanning "De Booner Vliet," the canal we called "De Vliet," our boerderij comes into view. It is often referred to as "De Lange Brug" (Long Bridge). I might pause a moment, taking in the view. At first glance, it appears to be surrounded by water. The building itself is large and almost entirely covered with a reed-thatched roof. The back part has a red tiled roof. The front of the building looks more like a barn than a home. True enough! Our boerderij's most unusual feature was that it was built backwards, with the cow barn facing the road.

I continue over the long bridge, then 50 meters further I turn left into our driveway and cross a bridge spanning a smaller canal. This canal flanks the road I have been on. Immediately to my left, there is a tiny island full of knotted willows. Ahead, I notice that the barge for cow manure lying in front of the barn is getting very full. I ride a little further, between an equipment garage on the right and a covered haystack on the left. Past the haystack, the three doors of the mid-section come into view (next picture). The first door, the one on the left, is our main entrance door. The second door is the stable door for our farm horse. The third door leads to what once was the threshing floor.

I have arrived home, but there is one more door into our home to view. This is the door at the back of the boerderij, facing the meadows. It is never used, but historically it was the front door of the boerderij. Now it opens into the bedroom where my brothers all sleep. A remarkable, original wood carving remains above this outside door. It depicts the Biblical story of the two spies returning with a giant cluster of grapes, proving that Canaan

was indeed a land of promise. This front door with its artistic, prophetic message is only seen by people who are invited to come admire the door's unusual, decorated gable. I've been told that no one knew why our particular boerderij, and only ours, was built backwards, with a manure pile facing the road and an inaccessible front door at its backside. I do know that this odd quality added to our personal sense of uniqueness as a family.

THE WEEK I was born was not a quiet one in the little town of Maasland. World War II was still raging in Europe and Allied bombers were flying overhead regularly to destroy German installations. By the end of 1944, the southern part of the Netherlands had been liberated by the Canadian army, but the rest of the country had remained under German occupation.

When the Germans cut off all food and fuel shipments to the western part of the country, many of the 4.5 million people in the region suffered from severe malnutrition. More than 18,000 people starved to death during what came to be known as The Hunger Winter. Two months after my birth, on May 5, 1945, the Canadian army was finally able to drive out the German forces and bring about the keenly awaited liberation of The Netherlands.

My uncle and aunt, Oom Teun and Tante Nel, lived in The Hague but due to the severe food shortages that winter, they had brought several of their nine children to Maasland to be cared for at our place and at my Tante Lena's. In his war-time journal, Oom Teun writes that The Hague was particularly hard hit that first week in March, 1945, and that smoke and an orange sky over the city could be seen all the way from Maasland.

Fast forward with me a moment to the summer of 1963, when I will meet a handsome young man named Adrian Guldemond, who would become my husband and life partner down the road. We were to discover that he was born on Jan. 11, 1945, just eight weeks before my birth and just 45 kilometers from Maasland, in the town of Boskoop. His family emigrated to Canada in 1956, just one year after we did.

My mother was able to feed me because as farmers in Maasland my family had sufficient access to food during The Hunger Winter. People in Boskoop fared far worse. Adrian's father had to steal out from under cover of darkness to go begging from farm to farm for a little milk, a little extra food for his wife, so that she could nurse her first-born baby. Adrian's mother later told me that of the 28 babies born in Boskoop that terrible winter, Adrian was one of only two babies who survived. As it was, he gained less than one pound in the first five months of his life.

It is amazing to me that given the tenuous start to his life, Adrian grew to over six feet tall and has been a very healthy, strong person for his whole life. I am thankful that I, too, have been gifted with a long life, in spite of being plagued by frequent illnesses. That March week in 1945, I was one of three grandchildren born to my maternal grandparents. Sadly, Uncle Harry and Aunt Mary's first child was stillborn. Oom Huib and Tante Aaf's fourth child, my favourite cousin Ria, lived for 12 years only. She died during the 1957 pandemic in Holland, the same Asiatic flu that made me so very ill in Canada. Of the three cousins, I am the only survivor.

May, 1945: I am the baby in this photo.

I REMEMBER MY earliest years as peaceful and unhurried. I had hours to wander about the house or to meander outside on my *klompen* (wooden shoes). Mostly I spent the days indoors, as it rained often or was too muddy or too cold out. Ours was a large home with very few rooms. If you could ask her, my mother would tell you that the house was old and impractical. Our entrance door led straight into the *"boen hoek"* (scrubbing or work area). This was the very large space in the mid-section of the boerderij where all the action took place and had taken place for two and a half centuries. Here water was heated in a primitive open hearth, and here the milk pails were cleaned twice a day. Here the weekly laundry was done, the cheese and butter were made, and the children were bathed. The water we used for cleaning and bathing and for the animals came straight from De Vliet. For human water consumption, there was a cistern collecting rainwater off the tiled roof of the equipment garage. Not so sanitary, either, as sparrows, starlings, and doves perched on that roof.

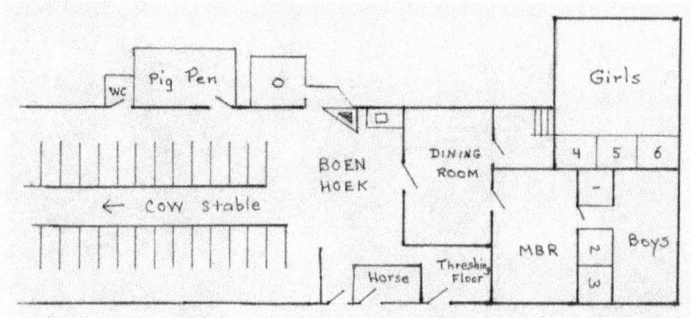

Boerderij Floor Plan

To the left of the boen hoek was the stable, large enough for 50 dairy cows. The boen hoek was never silent, not even in the evening, because there was no partition separating it from the stable. Gentle noises of cows breathing, eating hay, and chewing their cud were interspersed by the louder sounds of a cow mooing or a splattering noise after a tail went up. Muffled grunting of pigs in the adjacent barn could be heard. A barnyard smell permeated the whole area, but we were used to this. Against the wall opposite the stable was a kitchenette with a small counter, a sink with a cold-water tap connected to the cistern, a table, and a gas stove. In this kitchenette area, my mother and the maid prepared and cooked our food and washed the dishes.

A door near the kitchenette led into the room we called the "huiskamer." Its pot-bellied old stove made this the warmest room in the house. I will refer it as our dining room because a large wooden table surrounded by many wooden chairs dominated the room. Here we ate our meals, did our devotions, read books, wrote letters, and played with our toys. There was no living room, so this is where my parents regularly had coffee visitors.

Adjacent to the dining room was my parents' very large bedroom. In addition to their bed, a baby crib, and a baby dressing table, the room contained my father's roll-top writing bureau, my mother's striking secretary desk with hutch, and a stove to warm the room. I remember the room's beautiful wood paneling and its old, non-working fireplace with antique ceramic tiles.

The time has come for me to do a little truth-telling. The born-in-the-barn story I told earlier was a bit of a stretch, as the reader might have guessed. We were all born in this far-from-shabby bedroom, at least 10 meters away from the stable and the animals. Later I would learn that this room was once a formal parlor, not a bedroom at all. In the 18th century, homes in Holland typically did not have separate bedrooms. People slept in a *"bedstee"* (pronounced "bet-stay"). This was a bed in a deep wall closet which readily provided warmth and privacy. Sure enough, there were three bedstees on the north side of this paneled room (numbered on floor plan). I recall from my childhood that on several occasions my parents converted their big bedroom to a party room, restoring its original purpose. They just moved their bed to a corner and placed a few dozen chairs in a large circle around the room. Appetizers were served, the men smoked cigars and drank *"jenever"* (gin), and the women drank a little *"advocaat"* (brandied eggnog) or *"Boerenjongens,"* a spirited concoction made with raisins and brandy. And what did the children consume? I'm not sure, as pop or soda was unknown to us. I do know that the spiked raisins I begged to sample tasted really yummy.

To get to the boys' bedroom, we had to go through my parents' bedroom. When I was older, I understood how awkward this was for the boys. The girls' bedroom was in the opposite direction. We had to go through the dining room, into a hallway, and up a set of stairs to what we called the upper room. Below this bedroom was the cold cellar where we kept pork hams and other meats and many jars of home-canned vegetables and fruit. There were also shelves full of big round cheeses at various stages of curing. My mother was a skilled cheesemaker, and she sold these Gouda-style cheeses in the wholesale market.

On one side of our bedroom were three more "*bedstees*" (numbered 4, 5, and 6 on floor plan) one still intact and the other two converted to walk-in closets. The room seemed enormous to me, like a ward in a hospital, but it had only two beds in it. Decades later I had opportunity to visit my birthplace and I noted that the room had sensibly been converted to three smaller, separate bedrooms.

In my research for this memoir, I learned that this upper room was once the best room in the house. Oom Teun told us in his writings that when the boerderij was built in 1711, two stained glass windows graced this room on the north side, the same side where the unusual front door was found. Teun wrote that his father sold these windows to an antique dealer in Delft in 1911, and although they were wind- and weather-damaged, they netted him a nice watch. He described the stained glass as beautiful, depicting a scene that was reminiscent of a Jan Steen painting. Underneath the scene was an admonition in old Dutch, a little rhyme which basically means "Everyone should mind their own business."

Laat het volck boerten en gecken
Laat zes paarden een wagen trecken
Laat de zee ebben en vloeyen
Laat een yeder zich met het zijne bemoeyen

BEFORE I CONTINUE with my stories, I'd like to explain my habit of using the names Holland and The Netherlands interchangeably. Many Dutch people do this, although the country's official name is The Netherlands. "Holland" is easier to say, and I lived in the province of South Holland, so I feel that I have reason enough to say I was from Holland.

The Netherlands literally means "low-lying country." This is fitting because nearly half of the country was once swampland or below sea level. Over the centuries, Dutch engineers have skillfully dug hundreds of canals and created many polders (areas reclaimed from the sea) which are used for agriculture and other developments. Windmills or their modern equivalents are an absolute necessity in The Netherlands because the lowlands or polders lying behind the dikes need to be constantly drained to prevent flooding. In the old days this was the job of the millers managing the windmills.

When I was little, I did not know that during my father's childhood there was an actual, working windmill on our boerderij. Perhaps I did, but I had forgotten. When I began my research for this memoir, I learned that there once were 13 windmills in the small town of Maasland. Our windmill stood proudly next to De Vliet about halfway down our long and narrow farm. There it maintained the proper water levels in our polder's canals. The water in the smaller canals which ran through our fields and through neighbouring fields was at least two meters lower than the water in De Vliet, and up to five meters below sea level!

Regrettably, a fierce windstorm in 1929 caused the top of our windmill to come crashing down and break its blades. The windmill was then replaced by a diesel-powered pumping station. To appreciate the size of our windmill, pictured on the previous page, notice the haystack on the left and the woman near the center front.

As a child, I knew that the pumping station kept the fields from flooding, but not what happened to the water in De Vliet. Not until much later did I understand that in Maasluis, excess water from De Vliet was pumped up and into the "De Nieuwe Waterweg." This huge waterway connects the port of Rotterdam to the North Sea. It's all amazing Dutch water management and technology.

2. PRECIOUS MEMORIES

As a 4-year-old with my family in 1949 (Back row: Truus, Siem, and Tini. Middle row: Koos and Marie van der Kooij. Front row: Mieke (me), Corrie, Koos, and Jan.

Many canals, big and small, crisscross the landscape in the western part of the country. The roads I travelled as a child all seemed to be flanked by water. Not true, but water sure seemed to be everywhere, and this created a huge concern for mothers with little children. Surprisingly, youngsters were not supervised all that well. One of my cousins tragically drowned as a three-year-old. He had wandered off behind the house to look for his father working in their nursery.

My memory has it that we were not kept on a tight leash in our family, either. Little ones meandered freely outside. Occasionally there was a frightening episode when no one knew where one of us was. My panic-struck mother would always first run towards De Vliet while yelling loudly, "Help, help! … help find Japie! … (or Beppie, or Koos)!" If she did not see a child floating upside down in the water, her frantic search continued in other directions. There were many places to be lost on our big old property. One time the search went on very long and anxiety mounted. Jan was finally found, fast asleep in the tall grasses beyond the orchard.

We may not have been supervised all that carefully, but a very strict mealtime and breaktime routine governed our lives. At 7:30 am, we all had breakfast. It was the second breakfast for the men who had been up since 5:00 am or earlier to milk and feed the cows and the other animals. Older children went off to school and little ones were free to run around some more. At ten o'clock on the dot, everyone, children too, converged on the dining room for break time. I think this is when my mother did a regular headcount. My father, one or two farmhands, the maid, and my mother gathered for coffee, koek, and a chat. Fifteen minutes later it was back to work for everyone, and Mom and the maid started working on preparing hot lunch for the family and employees.

As I mentioned, the clock ruled our lives. For most of her life, Mom was most harried prior to mealtimes, nervous that when Dad stepped in the door, she might not have food on the table within 30 seconds. (Some of her daughters inherited this unfortunate trait. I, for one, had to learn not to feel like a failure if dinner was not ready for my husband until 6:15 pm.) After lunch, my parents went to bed for a nap lasting precisely 30 minutes. My mother always wore a better dress for the afternoon. At 3:30 pm, everyone gathered again for tea, and 6:00 pm was supper time. Its menu was very similar to breakfast: lots of sliced bread for open-faced sandwiches, Gouda-style cheese, jam, and *hagelslag* (chocolate sprinkles). Supper might include a few more options, like ham slices or sometimes a boiled egg. Children drank a glass of milk with this bread meal, adults had a cup of tea. (No drinks were served for hot lunch.) On long summer nights we sometimes enjoyed playing on the farm yard before bedtime. I have fond memories of playing hide-and-seek or kick-the-can with my older siblings and their neighbourhood friends when I was a little older. At 8:00 pm was the final coffee round for the grown-ups.

Weekend routines were a little different. Saturday morning coffee times were longer and more relaxed. My brother Simon helped me recall that we'd often have extra coffee drinkers and that it was "*gezellig*." (Dutch people cherish this word, but it's hard to translate. "Cozy atmosphere" or "conviviality" might do it.) Whenever they could manage it, the baker, the mailman, the broom salesman, and the veterinarian all made it a point to stop in at our boerderij at 10:00 am on Saturdays, just in time for a social visit over coffee. My father loved talking church news and politics with them, and my mother enjoyed getting caught up on news about the locals.

On Saturday afternoon a lot of water was heated in the "boen hoek" to fill the big metal tub standing ready for our baths. Then one by one we were all given a bath, starting with the youngest. Our mother washed our hair and firmly scrubbed us down, from behind our ears to between our toes. After adding some more hot water to the now scummy tub, we older children mostly took care of our own baths. The teens in the family gave themselves a sponge bath in the privacy of their own bedrooms.

I hinted earlier that there was something I didn't like about Sundays. It was the pressure to get to church on time. My mother was always tense as she checked up on each child or delegated tasks to make sure that everyone was dressed in their Sunday best. Truus or Tini had to make sure we had well-combed hair, and that each girl had a pretty satin ribbon tied into their hair. My father needed to compress all of his barn chores into a shorter time period. When he was finished and had cleaned up, he stood by the door, anxiously announcing how few minutes we still had. My mother hurried about, nervously trying to meet the deadline. If Corrie and I were ready early, she sometimes gave us bread crusts to feed to the ducks. Eagerly we'd head towards the small canal surrounding the little island. We could always find ducks here. As soon as we threw a piece of bread out to one duck, another dozen or so showed up, quacking loudly, begging for their own treat. One Sunday morning, as I tried lobbing a piece of bread farther to reach a lagging duck, I slipped down the grassy bank and into the muddy water of the canal. I managed to climb out, in tears of course, and soaked and filthy to my armpits. No church for me that Sunday!

I started going to church once I was old enough, likely five years old. Younger children stayed home because there was no childcare at church. I rode behind my mother or my father, sitting on their bicycle's baggage carrier. When I rode with my father, I remember listening with fascination as he exchanged greetings with all the other church-going men on the road. I tried to mimic their guttural, *"M-o-r-g-e-n, broeder"* under my breath, elongating the short "o" and making the "r" and "n" almost inaudible. It was the Maasland version of "Good morning, brother."

In the Gereformeerde Kerk (similar to Christian Reformed Church) in Maasland, men and women were still segregated in most of the church. Only in one section did families sit together. Most often I sat with my mother and older sisters in the women's section, but I loved it when occasionally my father invited me to sit upstairs with him in the men's gallery. From this vantage point, I could see most of the people in the church and I could look down on the ornate wooden pulpit which the dominee entered via a steep, spiral staircase. Fascinating also was the decorative Tablet with the Ten Commandments hanging very close to me. The one with the Apostle's Creed hung on the other side of the pulpit. I loved the calligraphy-style, gold lettering on black velvet. I don't recall much other art or ornamentation in the church. It was a Calvinistic church. When the men, all dressed in dark suits and ties, stood for prayer or to recite the Apostle's Creed or sing a psalm accompanied by the sound of organ pipes, I felt small but safe and secure beside my father. When we all sat down again, waiting for the sermon to begin, he gave me a peppermint and reminded me of my task. I knew it well. Whenever he'd nod off to sleep, I was to poke him. Sitting still on a hard pew and keeping awake was a challenge for many farmers. Fortunately for me, my father needed regular poking and time passed quickly in the church gallery.

Unforgettable were the times we went to church in our shiny black *"koets"* (carriage), pulled by our farm horse. That koets was parked in the equipment garage, and sometimes Corrie and I played in it. I don't think it was permitted, or we would have done it more often. The koets was magical to me. I remember stroking its soft, sage-green, corduroy upholstery and loving the feel of it. I'm not sure how imaginative our play was because we had limited cultural exposure. On the other hand, we might have heard a few fairy tales, and we did see some carriages at church.

The koets and farm horse were used whenever another baby was baptized, and that happened often. The koets was too small for all of us so the older children rode their bikes. I was only eight years old when Heleentje, our last Dutch baby, was born so I'm quite sure I still got the royal ride. My older siblings recall that when they were young, the koets was used more frequently, and that Tante Lena and Oom Wim took their horse and koets to church every Sunday to transport my paternal grandparents, Opa and Opoe. This was especially important for Opoe. She had never learned to ride a bicycle.

And who besides me and a few lucky young siblings were in the koets on those special days? The new baby and an adult, but not my mother. The baby would have been less than a week old, and leaving the house so soon after giving birth was considered too risky for the mother. But infant mortality was also a risk, therefore baptism could not wait. In a holdover from Roman Catholic practices, infants received the "seal of the covenant" as soon as possible. An aunt or an older cousin was given the honour of carrying the baby into church. We children looked on with pride as my father presented our new baby, dressed in an elegant white baptismal gown, to the dominee for administration of the sacrament. I remember coming home from church when Heleentje was baptized. Mom was overjoyed because she had been able to hear the service on the phone this time. The wonders of new technology! Mom was even happier when for the baptism of her last three children, the ones born in Canada, the event was delayed until the babies were two or three weeks old. She was able to join the whole family in church and she was finally an active participant in the sacrament.

MY MOST PRECIOUS memories with my father happened in Holland while he was milking. He'd be sitting on his one-legged stool, leaning his head against the belly of the cow, and rhythmically moving his fingers to extract the milk from the cow's teats, aiming the milk straight into the gleaming milk pail between his feet. It was not uncommon to find him singing a Genevan psalm when I entered the stable. He'd smile when he noticed me. Sometimes he asked me to recite my memory work for school, but we spent more time on counting and math questions. Dad was very good at mental math, and he enjoyed challenging me with problems to

solve. I remember one of these questions. I was perhaps six or seven. "How old will you be when you are half my age?" I pondered the problem long and loved the sense of accomplishment when I solved it. Mostly I chattered happily about whatever, and Dad was a captive, willing audience. I remember one day, when I was around four, he warmed my heart when he said to me, "*Jij bent mijn kleine lieve babbelkous.*" (You are my dear little chatterbox.)

My earliest conscious memory is of the birth of my brother Jim when I was three and a half years old. My father woke me late, a little after midnight, to take me to the potty. Then, with a huge smile on his face, he said, "I have a big surprise for you! You have a new baby brother. Let's go see him!" As he took me to my parents' bedroom, he continued, "You are the first person in the family to see the new baby!" Beaming, he showed me baby Koos. I was awe-struck! I lightly touched his tiny little cheek. I felt very special, and in a family as large as ours, it was not often that we felt special.

I remember my fourth birthday because my birthday gift was a very pretty, miniature china set. We had very few toys and this gift was unexpected and perfect. I spent hours with it and I remember happily serving tea to Corrie and Koos whenever they'd join me in my game.

Our family in 1949.

My brothers on our farm horse, with Adri, who was our live-in farmhand, when I was little.

When I was around four or five years old, my mother started sending me to Tante Lena with a *"briefje"* (note). She and Oom Wim lived nearby, at 29 Zuidbuurt. They were a childless couple and they looked after my grandparents in their last years. Tante Lena would scribble an answer on this piece of paper, and I'd return home with it. This aunt had a rather brusque manner but it was not her I feared, it was Opa, Dad's father. He often sat on a chair in front of the house and he always looked unfriendly. I'm not sure if he'd ever said anything unkind to me. It could be that my older brother, Jan, had teasingly warned me that if Opa saw me eyeing the pear tree in front of tante Lena's house, he would scold me royally for even thinking about eating one of those pears. Whatever the case, I'd breathe a sigh of relief if his chair was empty when I turned into the driveway. Happily for me, when I was around eight years old, a telephone was installed in our home. I did not mind losing my message girl job.

We didn't go away often; the way children do these days. We did not go to school until age 6. We certainly did not go to dance classes or swimming lessons or soccer games. The doctor made house calls. We did not go shopping with our mother unless she needed us for a fitting for a new coat, for example. Sometimes she'd take one or two of us along with her when visiting family, but most often she'd leave us at home with the maid or an older sister.

I don't remember being bored. There was always enough to do outside, too. I'd go see what the big people were up to or help Truus gather fresh eggs from the chicken coop. I might find Jan, playing with the fat rabbits on the grass near De Vliet. More often, I'd find Corrie and together we'd figure out some game to play. Often enough I would contentedly wander around, daydreaming and observing my world. The canal was always interesting. Sometimes a soft mist hung over its still water, other times the water was grey-blue with small rippling waves, and still other times the waves were dark grey, angrier. I liked watching groups of mallard ducks swimming in the canal and I was captivated by the richly coloured plumage of the male ducks. In the smaller canal I'd see ducks pecking at the green duckweed floating on the water.

The big canal, De Vliet, was the most interesting. I loved the gentle image of a pair of majestic white swans gliding by. Or a well-camouflaged blue heron, standing very still on the opposite bank of De Vliet, patiently waiting for its lunch. Herons love solitude. So did visiting artists. Our striking and picturesque boerderij nestling beside the canal was a magnet for artists, but they came one at a time and only during the warmer months. I watched with great interest when a new artist began settling his stool and easel on the reedy bank across the water. One artist sat in a little rowboat, right near the long bridge. I wondered how he kept his supplies balanced, especially when there was some wind. When these artists were busy painting, I wanted to watch them work, but alas, I was too timid to ask. When after a few days I'd finally find my nerve, they were invariably finished and gone.

Ria Kooij, Adrian's cousin, made this pen-and-watercolour rendition for us in 1975.

MAASLAND WAS MY hometown, but the island of Rozenburg was my second most familiar place. It was my mother's birthplace and my Opa and several aunts and uncles lived there still. Mom visited her father and sisters quite often. When I was little, I got a ride on the back of her bicycle. She'd ride to Maasluis towards the big river I remember as "De Maas", but was more appropriately named "De Nieuwe Waterweg."

There, we waited with other cyclists and a few cars for the ferry to carry us across the river. I loved the sound of the fog horn as it approached the dock. Once the ramp came down, my mother walked her bicycle onto the boat while I stayed close by her side. When all were on, the ramp was pulled up and the fog horn sounded again. The loud engines started up, churning the water below, and I'd watch with fascination as the shore line began to recede from view. Turning my eyes to the other side, I'd notice that the ferry terminal on the island of Rozenburg was approaching rapidly. The fog horn sounded again and with a shudder, the ferry docked. The ramp came down, and all the people around us crowded towards it to escape. I climbed on the back of my mom's bicycle again, and we rode fifteen more minutes to her father's home.

Opa had retired and no longer lived on the farm. The house he now lived in near the village of Rozenburg was small but "*gezellig*." The centerpiece of the living room was the dining table with its plush table covering in rich reds and browns, reminiscent of a Turkish rug. There were a few simple dining chairs around the table but Opa preferred to sit nearby in one of the fauteuils with wooden arms. (There was a strong French influence in the Dutch language, so "*fauteuil*" was the name we gave to an armchair, just like I had a "*portemonnee*" to carry my change to church, and my parents had a "*portefeuille*" to carry bills.) On the buffet in this room were various items of interest for my young eyes. One item I much admired was a little glass snow globe, an ornament which belonged to my youngest aunt, Tante Truus. She was Opa's housekeeper until her marriage in 1953.

Occasionally Mom sent Corrie and me to a relative for a vacation and Opa's was one of the places where we sometimes spent a few days away from home. Whenever Tante Truus left the living room, I found it hard to resist picking up the snow globe on the buffet, turn it over, and marvel at the snowflakes falling softly over the pretty scene in the globe. One day I didn't hear her returning and she caught me in the act. It so frightened me I dropped the globe and it shattered into a thousand pieces at my feet. Understandably, she was very upset with me.

Opa seemed to enjoy our presence. We always looked forward to a game he played with us after his afternoon nap. He was a diabetic and while preparing to give himself an insulin shot, he rinsed out the syringe and playfully squirted us with water. We whooped with excitement as we tried to hide from him under the table so he couldn't reach us. We were always a little disappointed when after a few minutes he ended the game and gave himself the injection.

After Tante Truus departed for Canada, Opa lived on his own for 13 more years, simply and frugally. My mother told me, for example, that he refused to turn on his little oil lamp until it was pitch dark outside. He lived in the days before refrigerators and he hated to throw out and waste food. My mother thought many of his digestive problems in his later years were likely episodes of food poisoning.

We loved this Opa. I never knew my grandmothers as they both died in 1949 when I was still little. My father's father died in 1953. My mother's father in Rozenburg was special for me. He was fun and he took time to interact and play with us. Of all the relatives we had in The Netherlands after we left for Canada, Opa Jan was the relative I missed the most.

3. MY MOTHER'S LIFE STORY

Her fear of mice and rats, my mother once told me, dated back to the time when mice crawled around her head at night. I was a little incredulous when she made this comment, so she explained that the mattresses and pillows they slept on consisted of cotton ticking filled with straw, which was an attractive nesting and food source for rodents. As my mother told us the story of occasionally feeling something move through her hair, and then waking to the horror of seeing a mouse scurrying away from her pillow, she flinched and still shivered in revulsion.

My mother cycling in Maasland, a little one behind her.

My mother, Maria van der Kooij, or Marie, the name everyone called her, was born on December 10, 1913 on the island of Rozenburg. She was the fifth in a family of twelve children: Ridder, Aaf, Arie and Bep (twins), Marie, Jaap, Nan, Piet, Annie, Pie, Wim, and Truus. Four of my mother's siblings immigrated to Canada in the early 1950's: Arie, Nan, and Wim to Ontario, and Truus to Alberta and later to BC.

My mother's family in 1948, celebrating their parents' 40th wedding anniversary:
Back row: Wim, Nan, Truus, Marie, Pie, Jaap, Aaf.
Front row: Piet, Annie, Opa Jan, Opoe Trijntje, Ridder, Bep & Arie.

My mother's father, Jan van der Kooij (1884-1966), dreamed of becoming a school teacher so he continued his schooling beyond grade 6. His two older brothers, Piet and Pieter, made fun of his ambitions and taunted him with comments like "Who do you think you are? Better than us?" The story I heard is that a couple of years later, he'd had enough of their derisive comments and bullying. In a fit of anger, he threw away his study books. He became a farmhand for a farmer in Maasland. For years he saved his pennies carefully and was finally able to buy a small and humble farmstead in Rozenburg. His fiancé was not impressed with his purchase and broke off the engagement. Jan rebounded. He had met a sweet maid at a previous place

of employment and he now proposed marriage to her. Trijntje Verboon (1886-1949) readily agreed, and the marriage took place in 1908. (Note: not everyone had large families in those days. Jan's two brothers, remained bachelors into their old age. His only sister Marie married at a late age and had two children.)

My grandfather milked fifteen or so cows and grew a few cash crops, but it was a struggle for him to eke out a living. The stories my mother has told me of her childhood suggested a childhood marked by poverty and stress, one that required spunk and resilience to make it through.

My mother was easily frightened. Her brothers nicknamed her *"Bange Marie"* (Fearful Marie) and they liked tormenting her, she told me. One game they played when they found her on the swing was to push the swing so hard that she feared for her life. She'd scream for them to stop, but they wouldn't let up until she peed her pants. From the few stories I heard, life in the Jan van der Kooij home sounded harsh and not particularly loving. "Do your duty, work hard, and don't be a sissy!" were family mottos. A few of my mother's stories suggest my Opoe was a gentle soul, and that my mother felt sorry for her. Her father's manner while my mother was growing up was demanding and stern. When he was older and less stressed, the kinder part of Opa's nature surfaced.

In our family album there was a small, black and white photo of my grandmother. She has knitting in her hands and is wearing a black dress with a white lace collar. Her thin white hair is pulled back tightly, presumably into a small bun, and with her sunken mouth, she looks old, very old. I was very surprised to learn some years ago that my mother's mother was only 63 years old when she died, not several decades older as I had surmised. Thinking about the picture again, I am quite sure that she was toothless. That would fit with a story Mom told me. Her mother suffered much with toothaches. No surprise, given a subsistence diet and a dozen pregnancies drawing all the calcium out of her body. Dentists were not affordable for poor folks like my grandparents.

Mom told me how she would sometimes hear her mother moan and moan for days with an ever-worsening tooth-ache. "My father would finally lose his patience and say, 'Enough! I am pulling it out!' He'd order my mother to sit down, grab the kitchen towel from the hook, and with his thumb and forefinger, try to yank the offending tooth loose from its socket. My mother would start screaming! I'd run out of the house at this point. I could not handle watching my mother suffer like that."

I asked her what happened after that.

"Well," Mom continued, "Sometimes the screaming would go on for a long time, other times the tooth came out easier. I waited until things were quiet again and my father had returned to the barn. Then I would slip back in and I'd see my mother curled up in her bedstee in the living room, now sobbing quietly. I didn't know what to do for her." As my mother told me this story, I could sense how badly she still felt for her poor, dear mother.

This reminds me of another painful story my mother told me, this one about her own tonsillectomy. She was around 8 or 9 years old when she and a younger brother and sister all had to go to Delft to get their tonsils out. Their father accompanied them on the trip, which involved walking two kilometers to the ferry, crossing the river, walking another kilometer to the Maasluis train station, riding the train to Delft, and then the final short walk to the hospital. Mom told me how terrifying the surgical procedure was, done without anesthesia. When it was their turn, each child had to climb into the special chair, have a large bib positioned on them, then were told to open their mouth and the doctor snipped away their tonsils. Mom may have told me more details, like whether they were offered ice cubes to suck on afterwards, but I have forgotten them because the next part of her story was more horrifying to me. When they had all been snipped, they had to make the same journey home. This time there were three young children crying with pain, which only made their throats hurt even more. First the walk to the station, then the train ride to Maasluis, then the walk to the ferry. After they crossed the river and stepped off the ferry, Opa picked up his bicycle that he had left in the grass near the dock. Then, turning to my mother, he said, "Marie, you get the little ones home! I'm late for milking," and with that he jumped on his bike and quickly disappeared around the corner.

My mother sighed deeply as she told me what happened next. "I was in agony, my throat hurt so much! The little ones were wailing and moving very slowly. We had a long way to go, and I didn't think I could go further. I looked at the ditch beside the road and I just wanted to go lie in it. To curl up and die! But then I thought of the little ones. What would become of them if I did that? They might do the same. I was responsible for them, I needed to take care of them!"

With this new thought firmly in mind, Mom told me that she steeled herself and kept going. Eventually, she and the little ones could see their home in the distance. In front of the house stood their mother, waiting for them with a tin box in her hand, ready to offer them a sugar cube.

"The poor thing," Mom said to me, "It was the only consolation she could think of for us, but it was the last thing we needed or wanted."

MY MOTHER'S FORMAL schooling was limited to five years of education, from age six to eleven. A century ago, classroom learning focused extensively on rote learning and on copying of numbers and text from the slate blackboard. Marie developed a beautiful handwriting style which she retained to her dying days. Unfortunately, her desk was near the back of the classroom and she made many errors copying the lessons on her little slate. She earned the nickname of *"Domme Marie"* (Stupid Marie). Not until the beginning of grade 5 was it discovered that she was nearsighted and simply could not see the board. With her new glasses, she finally did well in school. Her success was short-lived. It was her last full year in school.

Taking care of a big family in those days was very labour-intensive and time-consuming, not possible to do without help. There were no modern appliances and conveniences. (For example, even when I was young, my mother did the laundry on Mondays, but in rainy Holland it often took until Wednesday or longer to get it dried, folded, and put away.) My grandmother continued to have babies and could not afford to hire help, so soon after she finished grade 5, my mother became her mother's assistant, in training for a real job.

By the time she was school-age, my mother had only one grandparent. Her paternal grandfather (Ridder van der Kooij, 1843-1901) died years before my mother was born. Her mother's parents, Arie Verboon and Aafje van den Akker, succumbed to the Spanish flu (H1N1 Pandemic) in 1918, dying just one day apart. They had just celebrated their 50th wedding anniversary earlier that year. That left my mother with her father's mother, Elizabeth van der Kooij Voogt (1853-1931), as her only living grandparent.

My mother's grandparents, at their 50th wedding anniversary

When my mother was no longer in school, she was occasionally sent out to a relative with a temporary need. Sometimes she was sent to her grandmother for extended stays. Mom did not like her Opoe much. She especially did not like her hypocritical piety. Mom told me that Opoe instructed her to be on the look-out for the dominee coming down the street. If she saw him, she was to tell her immediately and bring the Bible and her reading glasses to her. The old lady would then quickly compose herself at the table, put on her pious face and her glasses, open her Bible, and start reading under her breath. My mother's description of the scene greeting the dominee when he knocked and walked in for his regular visit to this widow was worthy of a Rembrandt painting.

A few years later, my mother had reason to dislike her Opoe even more. She had been sent to help Opoe again when she was around 14 or 15 and in between jobs. Opoe was a suspicious lady who kept track of everything, and she noticed that Marie's personal laundry showed no evidence of monthly menstrual stains. When the next month there was still no evidence of blood stains, she confronted Marie and accused her of having sinned and being pregnant. Marie was deeply hurt by this shocking accusation. She had not started menstruating yet, which by itself is a worry and a humiliation for a young girl – most of her peers had their periods for years already. (My mother was 15 when she got her first period, as was I - the females in my family have all tended to be late developers.) My own memory of this story is that Mom's Opoe started a nasty rumour. Some of my sisters think the harm she did was limited to confronting and falsely accusing our mother. Whatever the case, that harm was significant enough. For my mother to have to deal with this accusation by her own grandmother was appalling. I doubt that the old lady apologized.

When my mother turned 13, it was time for her to be sent out to work. Her father found a paid position for her as assistant maid on a farm on the other side of the island of Rozenburg. My mother found the transition from living at home to becoming a maid for strangers very hard. She was the junior person in a team of at least 4 servants tending to all the farm and house work. The days were long, starting at 6:00 in the morning and often going to 9:00 in the evening.

If I remember Mom's story correctly, there were no real breaks, other than sitting down briefly for meals. One night per week she attended Catechism class at church, which she enjoyed because there she met people her own age. The only time she was permitted to visit her family was one Sunday evening per month. She missed her family and one day she became so homesick that she decided to run away. I imagine that her younger sisters and brothers were happy to see her, and perhaps her mother was, too. Not her father. When he came out of the barn and caught sight of her, he reprimanded her with a very stern, "What are YOU doing here?" Permitting no backtalk or excuses, he ordered her to immediately get on her bicycle and to go back to where she belonged! My mother never ran away again. She did what she was told and kept out of trouble, most of the time. She learned to grit her teeth and to take what came her way. However, my impression is that her internal dialogue was far from submissive or compliant, most of her life.

My mother held a number of maid positions at various farms. Her last position was for Juffrouw (Ms.) van der Lely,

a farmer's widow who lived not far from Maasland. During the years that my mother worked for Ms. Lely (age 18 to 23), her social life improved. In addition to church attendance on Sundays in Maasland, she attended the weekly Young Women's Club. My father attended the Young Men's Club on the same evening in the same church. It was not long before Marie and Koos started taking a fancy to each other. My mother also attended regular meetings of the local Christian choir. (Reformed churches did not allow choirs or soloists to participate in worship services until later in the 20th century because worship services were to be for honouring God, not for admiring human talent.) In the weekly choir, my mother learned to enjoy singing hymns and to execute vocal trills as she sang the high notes. I remember sitting beside my mother in church and feeling some embarrassment when her voice was the only one trilling. Some of my sisters similarly recall that our mother always held her notes longer than anyone else.

During this time my mother made friends with a neighbor, the mother of a young family. Ms. Lely allowed my mother to take some breaks, during which she sometimes slipped next door to enjoy a cup of tea with her neighbour friend. After the birth of her third child, her friend became ill with a serious infection and died a few days later. This loss was very hard on Mom. She told me she was heart-broken, losing the best friend she had ever had.

My own research found that not until the mid-1800's did a Viennese doctor make the connection between dirty hands and deadly infections. In the nineteenth century, medical doctors and students were becoming more scientific in their approach and were performing autopsies regularly to advance their knowledge base. Many did not wash their hands before doing other tasks, such as delivering babies. The observant doctor in Vienna noticed that the mortality rate for new mothers was spiking badly, so he recommended a hand-washing protocol. It took many years for all doctors to take this advice seriously. Meanwhile, midwives did no autopsies in their spare time and their deliveries resulted in far fewer deaths.

My impression has always been that Juffrouw Lely had more "class" than the other farmers' wives my mother had worked for. Ms. Lely was more refined, *"deftig"* (proper). However, class did not mean much to my mother. She knew her place when she was around people from higher classes, but in her heart, she knew with certainty that before God, all human beings are equal. I cannot picture my mother ever groveling for favours from what she thought of as "uppity" people.

My mother told me a telling little story about Ms. Lely. She had once given my mother a small gift, a pretty, hammered tin box which had held sugar cubes, a luxury in those days. Ms. Lely had several of these little tins, and when another one became empty, she offered it to my mother as a gift. When my parents set the date for their wedding, after almost four years of engagement, my mother gave notice to her boss. The lady was not pleased and insisted that she return the tin box to her. As my mother recounted the story a half century later, she was still annoyed that this well-off boss had been so stingy and small-minded to demand back this tiny little treasure from someone who had so little.

I do think that my mother learned many useful skills from this lady, preparing her well for the next stage in her life. My sister Catherine tells a further story about this period in our mother's life. In springtime the grape vines on Ms. Lely's farm needed to be suckered. If Marie completed her household tasks quickly, she was allowed to join the workers who were suckering the vines. Nimble-fingered Marie earned a nice little stash of extra cash for her bridal trousseau during this time.

MY PARENTS, Marie van der Kooij and Koos van der Kooij, announced their engagement when they were 19 and 23 years old. The story had it that they were unrelated, even though they shared the same last name. Marie was from a poor family from the island of Rozenburg, and Koos was the 11th child of a Maasland family which was financially a bit more comfortable, though hardly affluent. My father had a sister, Huibertje, and a brother, Jochem, who also married a spouse with the same last name, but all were unrelated to each other. Years later, my father's older brother, Teun, became fascinated by geneology and before he died in his nineties, he recorded vast amounts of family and local history. He proved that these "van der Kooij" pairs were in fact all related, three to six generations back. My parents, Maria and Jacobus, were related four generations back because they shared great-great-grandparents, Simon van der Kooij (1753) and Trijntje Poot.

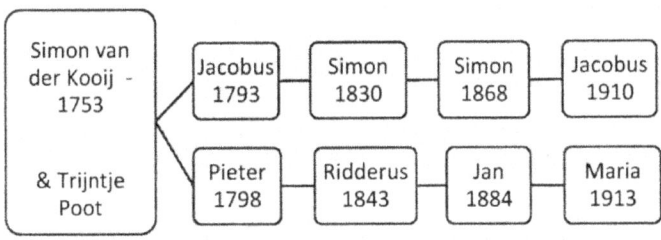

My father had seven older sisters to hover over him, and they were not so sure that he had made a good choice when he chose Marie to be his life's partner. She was only a maid after all, and she had no class status. Some of these sisters also worked in homes of aunts and others before their own marriage, but it would not have been as a maid. Theirs was an internship towards becoming a *"boerin"* (farmer's wife) and they would have enjoyed a higher status than the maids working on these farms.

At some point during the engagement, my father bought his love an engagement present, a stylish porcelain dinnerware set made in England. The sisters' tongues started wagging, my mother told me, because they thought Marie did not deserve to have such a beautiful set of china. My impression is that the sisters generally found my mother's attitude to be rather haughty and inappropriate. My mother, however, held her chin high and mentally thumbed her nose at them. She enjoyed her special china, and so did we. One of my special childhood memories, before and after immigration, was our Sunday evening meal. We carefully set a festive table with the blue and white, square luncheon plates. The larger platter held sliced bread (seen here) and the smaller serving dishes held an assortment of sliced cheeses and meats. When my mother passed away in 1995, exactly 12 pieces remained of her wedding china set, and we each received a piece as memory of our childhoods.

My parents were married in Rozenburg on May 4, 1937. Their wedding reception happened in a stable – in Opa Jan's stable. Cows in Holland were kept indoors only in the winter. In April, farmers let their cows and heifers out into the meadows to graze contentedly on tender new grass. (I have a lovely memory of watching my mother, both in Holland and in Canada, relishing the sight of young heifers running and leaping for joy when they were let loose in the verdant green pastures after a long winter of being cooped up inside.) Once the cow stalls were empty, the stable was thoroughly cleaned and all the walls were white-washed.

Family members helped my mother prepare the stable for the wedding reception. Boards were placed over the gutters to level the barn floor and tables were hastily erected on saw horses. Table clothes, garlands, and paper bells finished preparations for the festive occasion.

Selecting the wedding dress was another of my mother's less than happy memories. Her oldest sister had gone shopping with her to find a suitable wedding dress. On a clearance rack, Aaf found a dress made of blush pink satin. She had Mom try it on. It fit well and Aaf declared that she should buy this one. "It is only 5 guilders and it is good enough for you, Marie!" Sometime after the wedding, Mom learned that it was now in vogue for brides to wear white to signify virginity. Mom was embarrassed, annoyed with her sister for talking her into the pink dress. She was relieved that my oldest brother, Simon, was not born until ten months after the wedding.

My Opa and Opoe did not move out of the historic old home until the following year, so the newlyweds lived in a small, rented home. There was no honeymoon. The day after the wedding, Opa sent a message to my father at 5:00

am to tell him that he was urgently needed for morning milking because *"De knecht is ziek."* (The farmhand is sick).

That first year of marriage was not easy for my mother. At previous employments there had always been a team of at least two men and two women to do all the work. Now, as a married woman, Mom was a team of one. She had to get up at 4 am to get the wood stove started and to make tea and a sandwich for my father's first breakfast. There was no farmhand to keep the pile of wood behind the stove replenished and to look after a myriad of other chores. That all changed when my parents moved to the boerderij at De Vliet, the one where I was born. As farmer's wife, my mother had personnel to help her, but her workload also increased significantly. She was responsible for meal preparation for all (4-6 persons) who lived and worked at the boerderij, for making of butter and cheese, cleaning of the milk pails, general house-keeping, laundry, mending, and spring cleaning, which included whitewashing of the lower outside walls of the house. In the meantime, there were my mother's many pregnancies. By the time I was born, their fifth child, my parents had been married just eight years.

When I started writing this memoir, I did not know much about those first years of their marriage but my brother Simon and sister Catherine filled in many gaps for me. Earlier I mentioned that my mother was not too impressed with the old boerderij. Simon told me that one detail my mother was particularly determined to change was that horrible entrance into our home! Right into and through the horse stall. Illustrating the problem is best done with the photo below, likely taken in the late 1920's.

Oom Teun, sitting on the barrel, is visiting his parents and two of his sisters are hanging over the half door leading into the horse stall. The door to the right led into the threshing floor room, and I don't think that door was ever used. In my time, the space was a bedroom for the farmhand. There was no other door, so the only way into the house was past the farm horse with its swishing tail! This was so for family, for service people, and for important visitors like the doctor or the dominee. Simon pointed out the shallow trench in the cobblestones in the photo, allowing the horse's urine to run out and away from the building and then via a left turn to run towards the grass in the foreground. Visitors had to deal with this, too. My mother, ever resolute and resourceful, had a solution, although it did not happen until after the war was over. She had an extra doorway made to create a slightly more respectable entry into the mid-section of the boerderij. (Note extra doorway in photo, page 10, taken much later.)

WORLD WAR II figured large in the early years of my parent's marriage. For the Dutch, the war began when German forces invaded The Netherlands on May 10, 1940. The years of German occupation that followed became increasingly nerve-wracking. A half million able-bodied Dutchmen were transported to German factories for forced labour. Many of them never made it home. Worse was the persecution and deportation of Jewish people to concentration camps. Many Dutch people were actively involved in the resistance movement. My family also helped to hide "*onderduikers*" (literally, underdivers): Jewish people, resistance fighters, and others whose lives depended on staying hidden. If caught, they were often shot.

Simon, who was between two and seven years old during the war, recalls that sometimes there was a stranger at our breakfast table, a person he was to call "uncle." The uncle would often be gone a day or two later, but a week or month later there was a new "uncle" at the table. Simon also told me that a German sympathizer managed the pumping station where the windmill once stood on our farm. He could not be trusted. This added to our family's constant wartime dread.

Family lore has it that my father couldn't tell a lie if his life or the lives of others depended on it. This fact made my mother panic whenever German soldiers showed up to look for onderduikers at our boerderij. One of those times, when two onderduikers were hiding in the big hay pile stored above the cow stable, my mother managed to intercept the soldiers as they headed towards my father to interrogate him. She offered to take them around and succeeded in diverting their attention from the hiding place. At a cost. She was almost four months pregnant, but her fright was so bad, she told me, that she miscarried that same night.

One day my father had a close call. He had a calf slaughtered and had not reported it to the authorities because they would have confiscated it. He hid the meat in a special, ingenious hiding place which we had up in our attic. When soldiers showed up for a random, or not so random, inspection, the meat was found, and my father was taken to the local jail. I'm guessing that it was my father's awkward nervousness that gave him away. I have tried to imagine the state my mother would have been in that night. Talk about worry and fear! Thankfully, my father was sent home the next day with only a reprimand.

My mother with three little ones, sitting on the dock next to the Vliet, peeling potatoes. Note all the fat rabbits nearby.

4. MY FATHER'S LIFE STORY

A simple event can change the course of a life. In 1890, a farmer wanted to shoot a pigeon, shot himself in the leg, and died. Old Sijmen van der Kooij, my great grandfather, saw an opportunity and made an offer to his young son, Simon. "If you want to get married, I know a farm for you. If you cannot manage the finances, I will help you."

So it was that my grandparents, Simon and Kaatje, started married life and raised a family at the picturesque boerderij in Maasland where I myself would later be born.

My father, Koos, was their 11th child. He was born in 1910 and had eight sisters: Ka, Co, Lena, Huibertje, Maartje, Clazien, Anna, and Corrie, and four brothers: Siem, Teun, Jochem, and Niek. Three of the sons became farmers and most of the daughters became farmer's wives.

My father as a 5 yr. old in 1915, hand on his father's arm.

In the previous chapter I recounted stories I learned first-hand from my mother. My father was not a story teller, but I know a lot about his family, as will soon become evident. First, I will tell a little about the aunts and uncles I got to know best or are noteworthy for my memoir.

Tante Lena (1898-1993) was 12 years older than my father and she looms larger than the other aunts in my childhood memories. She lived just down the road from us, and she was the sister-in-law my mother had to contend with most often in the first 18 years of her marriage. Unhappily for my father, my mother and Tante Lena did not like each other very much. Tante Lena was a take-charge person with an overbearing personality who made it clear that Marie was the junior person in this family. Lena was prone to making tactless comments and was not subtle in her demands. For example, if her own maid was sick, Lena told my mother to send her maid over. My mother resented being treated with little respect and was not one to hide her irritations. Behind her back, and for many years, my mother muttered countless disparaging remarks about this aunt.

Ten years after we immigrated, Oom Wim and Tante Lena made a lengthy visit to our family in Simcoe. We became acquainted with another aspect of our aunt when she cheerfully conversed with us and showed a keen interest in each of us. She was curious about all things agricultural, church, and Christian organizations, recording many details in her trip's little journal, which my sister Magdalena has inherited. Lena recorded every little outing they took with my parents, every cup of coffee she enjoyed with a myriad of Dutch-speaking acquaintances. When she met Jerry, the baker, and Mrs. Bowland, in whose house I was boarding during my first years of teaching, she found it incomprehensible that they did not know a word of Dutch. Both Wim and Lena proved to be very helpful in the house and on the farm. Mom had been a little nervous about their long visit, but towards the end, she and Lena each remarked that the other person had become much nicer than they had remembered.

My father's sisters in 1945: Maartje, Corrie, Anna, Lena, Clazien, Huibertje, Katrien

Of all my many aunts, the only one in Holland I remember paying attention to me was Tante Huibertje (1899-1976). I remember her as kind and affectionate. She and Oom Jan lived on a farm on the other side of Maasland, and sometimes Corrie and I stayed at their house for several days in the summer. Tante Huibertje liked to joke around with us, especially during our bedtime routine. When we were all ready for bed, she'd kiss us on the cheek and give both of us a warm hug while whispering sweet things in our ears. After she left the room, we made some fun at her expense, dramatically wiping the wet kisses off our cheeks. Truth be told, she was the only person who kissed us. Or hugged us. Perhaps my memory fails me, but I do not remember Mom or Dad hugging or kissing us. If they did, it must have been a rare occasion. When I was young, our bedtime routine was: go to the bathroom, wash your face, put on your pajamas, give your mother a kiss, your father, too, if he is present, say your prayers, and go to sleep. We planted the kiss on their face, and they might have smiled, but the kiss was not reciprocated. It was my last job before going to bed and it did not feel like a sign of affection. I am still grateful to Tante Huibertje for offering another dimension to a kiss.

Oom Niek (1912-2001), number 12 in this family of 13 children, was one of the two chartered accountants in the family. I remember him as formal in his manner. I know little about him, but I am grateful to him for initiating the "rondzendbrieven," the letters which my father's siblings sent to each other and to their aging parents from 1940 to 1966. When this family letter arrived in their mailbox, each family read it, added their own contribution, and sent it on to the next family. When it was returned to him, Oom Niek

started a new one, but he sent the finished letter around one more time before archiving it. The brothers and sisters wrote 157 of these round-robin letters. They stopped in 1966, when telephone use was cheaper and when they all had cars for easy visiting.

After Oom Niek died in 2001, his daughter Cora, with help from a number of cousins, transcribed all these hand-written letters and published them in 2004 as five small books, 150 pages each. The letters are now a wonderful treasure trove of rich family history! Reading through some of these family letters again was fascinating. In the early letters, written during the war, they discussed food shortage, how to share rations, how to preserve nutrients by cooking potatoes with the peels left on, etc. A common thread in the letters was their positivity, their support and care for each other, and their readiness to express their trust in God and their gratitude for His gifts.

Of all my uncles, I found Oom Teun (1901-1994) the most fascinating. When I was little, his formal, citified speech patterns intrigued me. He sounded really competent and decisive. My mother thought he was too full of himself. My father and Teun got along very well and we saw him more frequently than my father's other brothers. That may also have been due to Opa and Opoe living down the street from us at Lena and Wim's place, and that Wim was his wife's brother. Teun helped my father manage his financials during the emigration process.

On our first trip back to Holland in 1975, Adrian and I visited with Oom Teun and Tante Nel in The Hague. Teun was a great host and his vast knowledge on a wide range of topics was impressive. He showed us his extensive bird egg collection, explaining that this was still a legal hobby when he was young. He took us shopping for authentic Delft blue pottery and arranged for Adrian to give us a mini concert on the big organ in a Delft cathedral. We found this uncle to be a very gifted person with boundless energy and drive.

My father with his brothers: Niek, Jochem, Koos, Teun in 1945

Teun's greatest gift to his extended family was the extensive research, writing, and publishing he did during his senior years about the family and town from which he came. I own a number of his books and booklets and have found them to be wonderful primary sources for my writing. He was 89 when the last of these was published. Thankfully, I can still read the Dutch language.

TEUN PUBLISHED a revision of his *"Familie Register van Simon van der Kooij en Catharina van Vliet"* in 1983. This

60-page booklet briefly records my family history to twelve generations back, beginning with Pleun Michielz van der Koij, born in 1557. Next were Gabriel, born in 1598, Jacob, born in 1628, Gabriel, born in 1668, Symon, born in 1694, Ridderus, born in 1723, and Simon, born in 1753. Striking for me was how old some of these forefathers became. This Simon was 88 when he died. Gabriel, born in 1668, died at age 91. Except for the first two, Teun also records the names of the wives of my forefathers. He provides more detail for the next generations, beginning with my great-great-grandfather, Jacobus van der Kooij (1793-1872). In 1988, Teun published *"Moeder's Jonge Jaren,"* and it provides extensive detail about his mother's family as well as his own family, which is, of course, also my father's family.

Before I continue with the stories told by Oom Teun, I will add a note about the historical context in which my great-great-grandparents lived. Their childhood occurred during the winds of change brought about by the French when Napoleon invaded Holland and much of Europe (1795). During the next 18 years, Napoleon brought modernizing reforms into Holland. He instituted a land registry and a national population registry, for which everyone without a last name had to choose one. The decimal system was adopted, and riding on the right side of the road became the rule. Representational democracy was established, although only rich men could vote. The universal right to vote would not happen for another century. The Reformed church lost its standing as sole and official church and the Roman Catholic church and Judaism attained equal status. The French period ended when Napoleon was defeated in 1813, but its reforms endured in Holland.

Teun writes that in 1809, Jacobus (or Koos, as he was known), began running a farm at age 16 for an elderly widow in Zuidbuurt, Maasland, the exact same road where I grew up. At age 34 he married Maartje van der Spek, a widow with 5 children. Koos and Maartje farmed the boerderij "*Middenhof*," inherited from Maartje's first husband. Together they had one child, Simon, also known as Sijmen (1830-1916). Oom Teun comments that Koos was active and involved in his community, but not someone to draw attention to himself. This was in sharp contrast to his son, Sijmen, who would become my great grandfather.

Sijmen van der Kooij was a prominent and colourful personality in the local church and community. A 1981 article in "*Trouw*," the national newspaper, describes my great grandfather as a "*rechtlijnige dwarsligger*" (inflexible contrarian) and a "hothead." The article cites as source my oom Teun's newly published book about Maasland, "*Dorp in Rust en Onrust*." One story describes how Sijmen made a scene when the town council asked visitors to leave so they could discuss a particular point in camera. Sijmen refused, claiming that as a citizen he had the right to stay, and that the Bible states that "*die kwaat doet, haat het licht*" (Those who do evil, hate the light). The article offers him a back-handed compliment, suggesting that he was an "*actievoerder*" (a man of action), the kind of people needed in this world to make changes. In another booklet written by Teun, the one about his mother, I learned that Sijmen was indeed active in society, whether it was as tax assessor, running for town council or church office, or to stop the mayor from cutting down trees along a certain road. In 1866 the first Christian school society was established in Maasland, and Sijmen was chosen as the first chair of the board. (Considering my and

Adrian's lifelong involvement in Christian education in Ontario, I found this tidbit fascinating!)

Conflicts were common in Sijmen's life. From Teun's writings, I gather that Sijmen was a difficult man with very strong convictions, childlike in his honesty, and lacking totally in diplomacy skills. Sijmen belonged to the *Hervormde Kerk* (Dutch Reformed Church) in Maasland until he left that church in a huff in 1882. A deacon had bought tickets in a lottery, then according to Sijmen, lied about doing it. Sijmen was deeply offended that the church council did not discipline the deacon appropriately. He stayed at odds with the church in Maasland, no longer attending church there, but continuing to write letters of complaint for many years. Teun tells us that when his grandfather was 85, a few of his children came over to discuss some needed arrangements. When they could not agree, old Sijmen banged his hand loudly on the table to stop the discussion, saying, "*Ik ben hier praeses!*" (I preside here!) A few hours later he died.

MY GRANDFATHER, SIMON (1868-1953), was the eighth and youngest child of Sijmen and Jaapje Zeelenberg. As mentioned earlier, when the boerderij at 5 Zuidbuurt became available in 1890, Simon was able to plan marriage to Catharina van Vliet (1870-1949), also known as Kaatje.

They had solved one problem, where to live and make a living, but they also had to solve a church problem. Their wedding happened during the height of the "Doleantie," the major church schism led by Abraham Kuyper. He objected to the liberalizing practices in the Hervormde Kerk and formed a new church, the Gereformeerde Kerk. The bride was still Hervormd, but many in her family had already joined the break-away church, as had the groom and some of his family. To prevent a serious family rift, the wedding took place in the bride's home and the officiant was the bride's uncle, Dominee Maan. After the wedding, Kaatje took catechism classes and became Gereformeerd, too.

My father's parents: Simon van der Kooij and Catharina van Vliet

Abraham Kuyper, a neo-Calvinist theologian and journalist, also promoted new ways to practise one's faith through the establishment of non-denominational Christian organizations. Later, as a successful politician and Prime Minister, he succeeded in establishing religious pluralism in The Netherlands. This ensured the survival of the Christian schools.

My father, Koos, was one of the youngest children in the family and he grew up during the post-Kuyperian period, when all kinds of Christian organizations were going concerns, for example, a Christian radio station, a Christian newspaper, and a Christian farmers association. I picture young Koos as a keen and conscientious participant in catechism, church clubs and Christian organizations. In his teens, my father took a public speaking course which trained young men to speak up in meetings and contribute to discussions in meaningful ways. It was a benefit to him for his whole life. I was present at some membership meetings which my father attended as member or board member, and I noticed that he spoke up regularly. He served on many boards and church councils during his lifetime.

At this point, I will tell a little about my grandmother's family. Her family story is both fascinating and tragic. Teun writes that when he was growing up, he knew that his mother, Kaatje van Vliet, was from a large family and that his grandfather, Teunis van Vliet, had died at the young age of 49, leaving behind his wife (Catharina Maan), a widow at age 45, with one son aged 13 and thirteen daughters aged 2 to 22. My grandmother, Kaatje, was just nine when her father died of a serious, short illness.

When Teun began poring over birth registers and other documents later on, he was very surprised to discover that his grandmother had given birth, not to 14 children, but to 19 children! Five more babies had died very young, between 5 and 14 months of age. Three just before, and two right after Kaatje's birth. What really surprised Teun was that his mother had never spoken about these dead children. When I carefully read Teun's genealogical list for his grandparents' family, I found another surprise. My great grandmother had 19 children in only 19.5 years! One set of twins. Eight babies were born just 11 or 12 months apart! Incredible! After her husband's premature death, my great grandmother apparently managed fine. Teun remarks that Widow van Vliet Maan was known by people as a strong but difficult woman. Her farm was far from poor, and her daughters provided free labour. Extra daughters were sent out to work as maids and most of them married young.

I HAVE ALWAYS been curious about my family's medical history. I found my Oom Teun's detailed accounts to be very helpful. As a true accountant, he is meticulous in noting specific details, often down to the last fact or to the last penny in an estate's inventory. If there is something negative to report, and if his evidence warrants it, Teun will say it, but he says it with care and sensitivity.

When I was young, I heard rumours about there being a history of mental illness in my family. Indeed, in the family of Catharina Van Vliet, my father's mother's family, mental illness does occur. Teun describes his mother Kaatje as *"evenwichtig en niet neerslachtig, wijs en rustig"* (calm, composed, and wise, no tendency towards depression) and he comments that this is in contrast to some of her 12 sisters and her only brother, Klaas. Teun writes that Coba and Klaas suffered much from "melancholy and depression" and that they were admitted to a mental hospital. In my sources, he does not say when, or how long. It seems a few more of my grandmother's sisters might have had some depressive tendencies but Teun is less clear about them. Her sister Kee had a severe intellectual disability and at age 20 was admitted for care in an institution. Her sister Lena died at age 23 during the birth of her first child. Another sister, Klazina, fell in the water while rinsing cheese-making cloths in a canal. She could not swim and drowned. She was 19.

If using a modern mindset, one might wonder if Klazina was depressed, if her falling in the water was a suicidal act. I think not. Few people could swim in the nineteenth century and as far as I know, suicides were rare. Most everyone in these small, rural towns believed in God and the Bible, and a very strong deterrent was the firm belief that hell was the destination for someone who committed suicide. I believe Oom Teun when he states simply that his aunt Klazina died because she fell in the canal. Also, that his brother Siem's death was a tragic accident, not a suicide, a story I will soon tell.

WHILE FARMING SEEMED to be in the blood of many of my forefathers and mothers, only one of Sijmen and Jaapje van der Kooij's eight children became a farmer or farmer's wife. That was Simon, my grandfather. This fact might help to explain why old Sijmen kept showing up on his youngest child's farm, meddling and interfering in all decisions, telling him which cow to sell and when, etc. The way Oom Teun tells it, Old Sijmen was a successful farmer who managed his finances well enough to withstand adversities. My grandfather was still a child when one morning, eleven cows in a row lay dead in their stalls. A few days later, all the cows were dead. Sijmen was able to survive this outbreak of *"veepest"* (cattle plague) and buy new cows to replace the dead ones. According to Teun, his father was less confident, less successful than his grandfather. "My father lacked in independence. He was somewhat interested in modernizing operations, but he didn't have what it took. He preferred to stick to old-fashioned ways."

For a while, my grandfather became financially a little more comfortable. The Dutch stayed neutral during World War I, and the Germans bought up all the farm products they could, so farmers did very well in the 1915-1917 period. This made it possible

for my grandfather to buy the boerderij he had been renting since 1890. He also bought himself some luxuries, Teun writes, like a fancy new carriage and horse. This might explain an old photo I'd always wondered about, a photo of my father and his younger brother, Niek, in which they looked to be about 7 and 9 years old. Posed carefully with their goat and goat cart at the entrance to our neighbours' beautifully treed lane, the young boys looked like well-to-do kids! The good years did not last. Making mortgage payments became more and more difficult, and in the 1930's my grandfather had to sell the farm and rent it back from a new owner.

My father, Koos, was given opportunity to become a professional like two of his brothers who became chartered accountants. However, at age 14 he dropped out of school, having decided that he preferred the familiar family vocation of farming. He started working fulltime for his father. Five years later, his oldest brother, Siem, died. Teun writes that Siem liked visiting his aunts and uncles on other farms whenever he had a day off work. On February 3, 1929, there was a strong frost and the next day Siem took advantage of the frozen canals to take a shortcut to visit two of his uncles. As he skated through isolated back farm country, he hit a soft spot in the ice where De Vliet meets the Bommeer Lake. Siem could not swim and he drowned. According to Teun, the thin ice had not been noticeable and was in part caused by ducks which had kept the area from icing over the day before.

Losing his brother at age 18 must have been painful for my father. Siem was 36 and he was his father's main helper on the boerderij, so Koos and Siem would have done a lot of farm work together. To my knowledge, my father never talked about the losses in his life.

By the 1930's, my father had become the designated son to take over the family farm. Two brothers were accountants and his other brother, Jochem, was already married and on a farm in a new polder in North Holland. That left Koos. In 1937 my parents were married and the following year they took over the farm from my Opa and Opoe.

My father's parents in their retirement years (1943)

In 1939, when he was 29, my father suffered another personal loss. His older sister, Tante Co, worked for relatives in her twenties but for health reasons returned home at age 30. She was in charge of cheese-making until she became ill with tuberculosis. She was 43 when she died.

My father had worked alongside this sister for many years, and he took her loss very hard. He knew that TB among the cows was the likely cause of her death, and he determined to eradicate TB in his barn. In his father's barn, ill cows had been kept far too long. Other farmers were modernizing their watering and feeding systems to minimize spread of the dreaded disease, and my father set about doing the same. In a building as old as ours this was no mean feat, and it took a few years before the annual inspection of his herd finally yielded a TB-free certificate. My father was overjoyed!

THERE IS A LITTLE MORE to tell about my Oom Siem. From family lore I'd picked up vague hints that there was something different about him. I learned much more from Oom Teun's writings. He gently describes his oldest brother as having some social and behavioural differences. He had *"een zekere beperktheid"* (some limitations) but no academic difficulties at school. He worked on his father's farm and loved horses, kept ducks, and enjoyed carpentry projects. He read the newspaper and read many books (unlike his father, who read the newspaper but had little use for reading books). Teun reports that Siem's extensive collection of books numbered 70 when he died.

Siem did not go to church because he thought people were looking at him too much. However, he would not tolerate any criticism of the church. He didn't like city folk because, according to him, they spoke *"verkeerd"* (the wrong way). Teun writes that Siem's behavior was sometimes obstinate or difficult. Respectfully, Teun chose not to elaborate. He gives the distinct impression that Siem did not fit in well socially and that cognitive rigidity was a strong trait. He also hints that Siem had experienced bullying: "He had not experienced everyone's respect or esteem in his life." At his funeral, the dominee remarked that the *"samenleving"* (social life) was difficult for someone like Siem, who socially and behaviourally deviated from the norm. Teun writes that he very much appreciated the dominee's compassion and depth of understanding for his oldest brother.

MY REFLECTIONS AND SOME THOUGHTS ABOUT OOM SIEM

In the booklet, "Familie Register van Simon van der Kooij en Catharina van Vliet," re-published in 1983, Oom Teun speculates that his brother Siem was born with some neurological or genetic difference. If he had written this booklet 20 years later, I think he might have speculated that his older brother had Asperger's Syndrome (AS). Not until the 1990's did this term surface in medical literature as a way to understand people with a unique set of learning differences. Currently, Asperger's Syndrome is considered to be an autism spectrum disorder (ASD).

From the little I know of Oom Siem, I would hazard a guess that if he had lived 100 years later, he would have been identified during his school years as being on the spectrum. Current thinking has it that there is a strong genetic basis to Asperger's Syndrome. If Oom Siem had ASD, it wouldn't be surprising if one or more of his siblings or their offspring had it, too, to a greater or lesser extent.

Professionally, I have had significant experience with students who were somewhere on the autism spectrum. As a teacher and as a consultant in special education, I found it rewarding to work with students who had mild or moderate functional learning differences and to help their teachers learn to support them with greater understanding and compassion.

Why does this ASD question matter? It is my view that if we better understand how people with ASD, or ADHD, or dyslexia, or learning disabilities function, we can be more compassionate and less judgmental about some of the ways they behave. They, in turn, will suffer less.

I have wondered about ASD in my father's family. Common features of Asperger's Syndrome are cognitive inflexibility and social difficulties. My father and some in his family certainly had a strong tendency to black and white thinking and moralism. Rigid adherence to church doctrines and principles suited my father's need for structure and predictability. He was very focused on doing the right thing. He did not always read social cues well, and sometimes he made social missteps. He was very honest, honest to a fault sometimes, and he often felt duty-bound to admonish others if they made moral infractions.

What helped my father was that he had a stable and secure childhood in a small town where little had changed in 100 years, where rote learning was prized and where expectations were predictable and unambiguous. My father's saving grace was a calm and gentle spirit.

5. NO LONGER LITTLE

A few weeks after my 6th birthday, and with much trepidation and apprehension, I rode on the back of my mother's bicycle for my first day of school. In my small town there were no kindergarten or pre-school classes, so grade 1 was the school entry year for all of us. When we got to the school, I nervously got off and my mother parked her bicycle. I clung to her hand as we walked towards the main door through a gauntlet of jeering grade 2 and 3 students. They were yelling things, but I didn't understand what they were yelling and why. I clung more tightly to my mother's hand. She brought me to the grade 1 classroom, delivered me to my teacher, and disappeared.

Suddenly I was alone, without family. I sat in my little desk amidst strangers, quite petrified. I winced when the loud school bell sounded. The teacher put her index finger to her lips, indicating that we were all to be quiet. Then she introduced herself and explained the classroom rules. The most important one was that we were not to speak without permission. Pointing up, she said, "Raise your finger like this. When I give you permission, you may speak or ask a question."

When the teacher began her first lesson, I followed her instructions meticulously. Pointing to the big chart on the blackboard, she said, "Pick up your pencil, … now write an 'a' like this in your new notebook, …. Then add an 'a', then a 'p' …. This spells '*aap*' (or monkey, in English). She was teaching us the first words all Dutch children had been taught to read from the very beginning of the century. My parents, too. It was a very effective method, teaching vowel and consonant sounds in context of whole words, from the most common to the least common vowel sounds. As a past literacy and also special education consultant, I'd say the

methodology had a lot going for it. The beauty of the "*aap, noot, Mies*" program was the visuals and the consistent order of presentation.

As I write about my first day at school, I wonder if I knew how to write my own name. Probably. I don't remember having much if any paper in our home, nor pencils or crayons. I know for sure that my mother had only one pair of scissors in the house her whole life, and that she was constantly annoyed that someone had used it and not put it back where it belonged.

As preschoolers, Corrie and I regularly played family or church or school. I gave myself an authoritative role like mother or teacher, and Corrie usually volunteered to be father or dominee. We assigned Koos, and later Beppie, to the child or student roles. We liked telling the little ones what to do, but reading and writing was mostly pretend, as we had few if any tools. To the day she died, my mother happily used the back of envelopes to write messages or to make lists. I must be getting old - I have started doing this myself.

On that first morning in school, I can still remember the relief I felt when the noon bell rang and it was time to go home for lunch. I do not recall if I walked the two kilometers home on my own, or if my sister Tini took me home on her bike those first few days. I know that after that first day, my mother no longer escorted me to school. Once home, we hurriedly ate our hot lunch. After my father's Bible reading and prayer, the school-aged children dashed off to get back to school in time for afternoon classes. I was now one of them. My leisurely, pre-school life had evaporated and had become part of my past.

I clearly remember the first day of school a year later. I joined the grade 2 and 3 students flanking the walk near the entrance door as the new grade 1 students approached the school, nervously clutching the hands of their mothers. We mocked them, chanting a version of "Kindergarten babies, …" at them. We felt so big, so brave, and I liked being part of the initiated. Then I noticed the fear and apprehension in the eyes of some of the little ones. They looked like lambs being led to slaughter. It was then that I remembered my own fears of the year before, and I was ashamed that I had so easily succumbed to joining my peers in teasing the incoming students. The fun was gone, and I did not join the jeering crowd the following year.

Grade 2 turned out to be a good year for me, in spite of my negative anticipations. The teacher, Pie van den Akker, was a formidable and competent older woman who had taught most of the residents of our small town. Many parents were still a little afraid of her. My grade 1 teacher had been a new graduate who had always spoken reassuringly to us. Not Juffrouw (Ms.) van den Akker. She was a firm disciplinarian. I knew her by reputation and also because, as my misfortune would have it, I sat next to her and her sister in church. In the women's section, my mother had a permanent seat for herself and several daughters. Next to us were the assigned van den Akker seats. Even as a youngster, I knew that these ladies were spinsters, and that this word had a negative connotation. They had not achieved an important goal in life, which was to attract husbands. Never mind that the teacher had had a major, positive role in the education of most of the town's people! Sitting sandwiched tightly between the women and girls in our pew, I sat as quietly as I could, lest I draw the negative attention of my future teacher.

My grade 2 school photo, with brother Jan

Grade 2 lessons were much more interesting. In grade 1 we had learned to do math, to read, and to print words and sentences. Now we learned to write cursively and to study content subjects like science, history, and geography. I remember memorizing the names and locations of the Dutch provinces and cities. Weekly art classes were new and exciting. The teacher had a set of 50 pictures which she sent around the classroom and we could choose a new picture to copy each week. Exact duplication, not creativity, was the goal. I remember drawing a tulip one week, a swan the next, and a windmill the following week. I excelled in the subject. Once a week there was a knitting class for girls only, so it was taught after school. While knitting socks was no longer a life skill, as we all wore factory-made socks now, knitting was still part of the curriculum.

One particular event in early grade 2 stands out in my mind. Lunch was not ready when we came home from school that day so we started eating later than usual. We knew for sure that we'd have trouble making it back to school on time when my father's Bible reading passage and closing prayer were extra-long. I remember grabbing my coat and running most of the way to school. The final bell rang as I threw my coat on the hook and totally out of breath, slipped into my desk. The laughter started, and before long, everyone was looking at me and laughing. I looked down, and then I saw it. My apron! In my rush after lunch, I had forgotten to take it off! I felt my face turning beet-red. To my surprise, the teacher I had so feared came to my rescue. Ms. van den Akker told the class a story of how she had been in a similar situation as a youngster – she'd forgotten to remove her bib before going to school. Her story worked. My classmates laughed at the novel thought that their teacher was little once and wore a bib. They were distracted, and I was comforted by my teacher's unexpected and sympathetic action.

HOLLAND IS THE LAND of "klompen" or wooden shoes. The klompen Adrian wore as a toddler were worn so well that the wood had grown very thin in places - note the long crack in the left klomp. Adrian's mother, who  was more sentimental than my mother, kept these little clogs and brought them to Canada in 1956 along with other treasures. I was delighted when she passed this keepsake on to me.

By the time I started school, klompen were only worn at home. To school we wore leather lace-ups. My oldest brother Simon, who was seven years old when I was born, has a different memory. Like almost everything else, leather shoes became unavailable during the war years. As their leather shoes wore out, all children started wearing wooden, locally made shoes. Village children, too, not just children who lived on farms. It took some time for the Dutch economy to recover after WWII, so Simon remembers wearing klompen for most of his school life. Leather shoes were reserved for church and for special occasions.

To my chagrin, I had to wear klompen for a couple of days in grade 1. Or was it in grade 2? My mother had taken my hand-me-down leather shoes to the shoemaker for re-soling, and I had no other pair of shoes. There I was, clomping along loudly in the school hallways, the only student wearing wooden shoes! I felt like a country hick. After school, I anxiously asked my mother if she had picked up my shoes.

"No, I had no time to go to Maasluis today," she said, without expression of regret or sympathy. I faced another day of embarrassment. I remember my relief when the day after that, I could go to school in leather shoes again.

I did not mind wearing klompen at home. We wore the plain kind, not the brightly painted and decorated ones sold to tourists. We started wearing them when we were very little. My whole family and the other farm workers all wore klompen outside and in the barn. Klompen suit the damp and cool Dutch climate – they are wonderfully warm, waterproof and safe for feet that might get stepped on by a cow or a horse.

As a child, I'd noticed all the "*knotwilgen*" (knotted willows) growing everywhere. In this photo, Corrie and I are enjoying a snowball fight in front of the small canal, the one I fell in while feeding the ducks on a warmer day. The island behind us is full of knotted willows. I thought these were strange-looking trees, especially when all their branches were cut off, leaving just their trunks. Later I learned what an amazing natural resource they are. Numerous new branches quickly grow again on their shaved heads. Simon told me that the trimming happened every five to seven years in our day. The smallest branches were dried and used for stove kindling, and the larger branches were tossed into one of our many small canals to soak. After six months the rotted bark easily peeled off, exposing beautiful, blond willow wood. This wood is very strong and water repellant, great for fenceposts and all other kinds of posts. So how are klompen made? You guessed it! Trunks of fast-growing willow trees are perfect for making wooden shoes!

IT WAS a special treat when my mother took me shopping to buy new shoes. I remember going with her to the shoe store in Maasluis as an 8-year-old, and being intrigued by the new X-ray machine the owner had just acquired. I tried on a pair of shoes, stepped onto the platform, looked in the viewfinder at my shoulder's height, and lo and behold, I saw the skeletal bones of my toes and feet illuminated in a ghastly green. The salesman gave my mother quite the pitch. No longer did she have to guess, she'd know for sure there was room for growth in these shoes. Listening to the squeals of other children as they kept stepping on the machine's platform to see their toes wiggle, I, too, thought it was a marvelous invention. The fun in shoe stores did not last long. A year or two later the machines were banned because the powerful radiation they emitted was no longer deemed safe.

Occasionally Corrie and I travelled with Mom by bus to shop in Rotterdam. This city was flattened by German bombs at the beginning of WWII, but by this time it had been re-built. I remember a 1953 shopping trip to "De Bijenkorf." It was our first experience in a modern department store. Corrie and I were especially intrigued by the escalator that magically brought us from one floor to the next. Coming down to the floor below, we noticed a crowd gathering near the escalator. Because of the congestion, Mom had no choice but to listen to the salesman demonstrating a new blending machine and making something he called mayonnaise. He handed out free samples. I was wowed by its delicious taste! At our home in Maasland, our meals were very basic and simple. Butter went on bread, and vinegar was added to beets and to cucumbers or lettuce in season. Other flavor additions were limited to salt, pepper, nutmeg, cinnamon, and sugar. Salad dressings and mayonnaise were not yet part of my taste experience.

While writing this memoir, I have been reflecting on how meal preparation was so different in my younger years. People in Holland had no refrigerators and most had no ovens, either. We did not bake our own bread, cake or cookies. The baker delivered bread to our door every day. If a treat was in order, we went to the bakery in town. In the grocery store, we asked the grocer for sugar, chocolate hail, factory-made coffee cake and cookies, and other food supplies. No self-serve stores yet. The butcher came to our door regularly to deliver various meats and cold cuts. After one of our hogs was slaughtered, we had lots of smoked ham and bacon in our cellar. On Fridays the fishmonger often stopped by, and on those days, we feasted on smoked mackerel or fried sole. Most people at that time had only a large hot plate on a counter. We had a proper gas stove, but my mother used its oven for utensil storage, not for anything else. To cook a beef roast or ham or to make soup, she used a large, enameled cast iron pot. I find it interesting that these multifunctional "Dutch ovens," which originated in The Netherlands in the 17th century, have become so popular in North America in recent years.

6. WATER, EVERYWHERE

Remember the story I told about Opoe in chapter 2, that she couldn't ride a bicycle? There was a reason. She was born more than twenty years before safe and comfortable bicycles were invented. When bicycles became popular, she was already married and having children. From the 1890's on, Dutch people took to cycling like ducks to water. Short distances, a flat terrain, and a moderate climate made a bicycle the perfect mode of transportation. Even today, the Dutch own three times more bicycles than cars.

Maasland, like many places in Holland, has lots of narrow roads flanked by canals. This can make cycling precarious and make watery accidents not uncommon. Some canals were only two meters deep, but others were considerably deeper.

Before I got my own bicycle, I got rides from the bigger people in my family to church, school, a store, or just for fun. I remember one particular day when I was sitting on the bicycle rack behind my sister Truus. My guess is that she was 10 or 11 and I was 5 years old. We had come from Tante Lena's and we were almost home. Zuidbuurt, the road we lived on, was narrow and barely wide enough to allow two-way traffic. Running along the side of this road was a 5-meter-wide canal. Vehicle traffic was still rare in the 1950's, but this particularly day a small truck came towards us from the opposite direction. As it sped by us, Truus swerved hard, lost control, and we toppled sideways into the murky water. The truck kept on going.

It all happened so fast. One moment I am happily hanging on to my big sister's waist, and the next I'm falling and going underwater in the canal. Frightening! The teenaged twins who lived on the opposite side of our road heard our cries and rushed over to pull me and Truus and her bicycle out of the water. As we stood there, dripping wet, Truus was understandably very upset. In an agitated voice she tried to explain to our rescuers that the truck had come by at high speed and that as it passed, the driver had opened the truck door to kick at her. I objected that I had not seen a truck door opening or a driver kicking. Truus insisted that was what had happened and that the driver had caused it all. Was she saving face? I kept quiet after that, just wanting to go home, put on dry clothes, and forget it all.

In the summer of my grade 2 year, I got my own bike. I remember my father asking me to sit on the bike, a hand-me-down from an older sister, to see if I could reach the pedals yet. I could not. Then he attached wooden blocks to the pedals. They were 5 cm. thick and clumsy, but I could now reach the pedals. I was delighted to have my very own bicycle and began practicing riding my bike in the farmyard. From then on, I rode my bike to school and back, five days a week, and to church on Sundays with the rest of the family.

I was not a confident cyclist. I remember often feeling a little nervous and quite wobbly. On my way to school one day in grade 3, a gust of wind caused me to fall and tumble into the canal beside the road, bicycle and all. A nearby adult noticed, and fished me and my bike out of the water. I have no memory of what happened next. Did this good Samaritan take me home, which was a half kilometer or more away? Or did I get back on my bike, drenched and all, to return home on my own? It was likely the latter, as the neighbourly person would have assumed that I could get myself home.

M. Guldemond, 2018

This memory reminds me of another story. It must have happened in grade 1 because I was walking home from school. As I started the long walk, my home-made underpants began to slip down. The elastic had sprung! Trying to hold up my panties through the layers of my woolen skirt and undergarments was not working well, and I had a long way to go. The panties kept slipping down further. I became more and more anxious, fearing that before long the panties would be lying around my ankles. I was still in town and I looked at the houses I was passing, but none were familiar. Finally, overcoming my natural shyness, I chose a house, walked up to its front door while still clutching my skirt, and rang the doorbell. A woman came to the door. In tears by now, I explained my problem to this strange lady and asked her for a safety pin. She excused herself a moment and returned with a pin. While standing on her stoop, I hoisted up my skirt, and she helped me secure the safety pin into my panties well enough to keep them up for a while. I thanked her and went on my way, much relieved.

My grade 3 school photo: Tini, Jan, Mieke, Corrie

TO BE COURAGEOUS or "flink," to face our fears, was a regular expectation. When I was eight or nine, my mother deemed me old enough to go on my own to visit my Opa in Rozenburg. I knew the directions well, but was filled with both excitement and trepidation as I approached the ferry dock. I was little, and I was surrounded by adults and older children waiting impatiently for the ferry to dock. As soon as the boat was secured and the ramp was down, everyone around me jostled to rush onto the boat. I pushed my bike forward, too, and noticed the tiny gap between the dock and the ferry. Worrying that the gap might grow larger,

I hurriedly pushed my bike onto the boat. I stood at the side while the last passengers came on board, and looking overboard, noticed the larger gap between the boat and the shoreline. I was mesmerized by the churning dark waters far below. The ramp went up, the fog horn sounded, and we were on our way. Ten minutes later, the ferry docked on the other side. This time, I told myself not to look at the gap between the ferry and the dock. I focused my mind on getting to Opa's home. It still surprises me that my parents let me go alone for this adventure when I was still so young.

Most winters it would freeze for a spell, enough for the canals to freeze over. If it did, we happily skated on the canals for at least a few days. I remember tying what we would now call very old-fashioned skates onto my shoes. Several winters it even froze enough for us to skate the two km. to school. At many of the bridges we had to climb up and around the bridge to avoid thin ice or open water under the bridge. In my memory, I am on my own, but nearby are many other children, heading in the same direction. The sun

is shining and there is an excited buzz in the air. I do not remember adults being around, keeping watch. They must have been around, but they certainly did not hover over us. I found this photo of Jan and me, stopping our skating to be photographed ... and an adult on the frozen canal behind us.

One cold winter we witnessed a spectacular event. As thaw was setting in, the ice was still thick but it had begun to crack and to develop a few holes. The ice cracks may have had something to do with water being pumped out of De Vliet at regular intervals in Maasluis. This winter something very unusual happened. Hundreds of gasping fish came to the surface in these holes. We younger children watched in awe as my father and older brothers walked onto the ice, pails in hand, then started grabbing the fish by hand and filling their buckets. Neighbours were doing the same. More buckets were found and filled with more dazed fish. What had caused this phenomenon? The theory was that the fish were oxygen-starved, possibly caused by gases emitted from the decaying vegetable matter at the bottom of the canal. Whatever the cause, we thought we were experiencing the Biblical miracle of the feeding of 5000. I think we ate more fish and eel that week than we normally did in a year.

MY MOTHER HAD many strong fears. Thunder storms scared her a lot. She winced visibly and made anxious comments if a lightning flash was closely followed by loud thunder. She scolded us severely if we stood too close to a window during lightning storms. Somewhere in my childhood I learned that lightning and thunder were God's angry voice, God's way of speaking to people. The more lightning flashed, and the louder the crack of thunder, the more it scared the child I was. I remember one storm being so severe that my mother pulled us around her and prayed aloud for God's protection and mercy.

When I was almost eight years old, there was a terrible winter storm that scared not only my mother, but also my father, and all the other adults around me. The dramatic Bible story of Noah and the Flood, the story about God punishing his people for not obeying him, was front of mind for me that weekend. A ferocious North Sea storm was making contact with land all along the coast on Saturday evening, Jan. 31, 1953, striking our low-lying country with a vengeance. The grown-ups around me all looked extremely tense as they prepared for the coming storm. Some were glued to the radio, listening for weather updates. Zeeland, the province consisting of many islands just south of us, got the brunt of the storm that evening. Sunday morning the gale winds had not let up. If anything, the storm was increasing in strength. Many dikes in Zeeland had broken overnight and many people and animals had drowned. Sunday afternoon the radio reported that there had been a second storm surge that caused even more casualties than the first. If more major dikes would be breached, much of our own province would also be under water. It was still raining very hard, and I could hear the willows bending and groaning in the wind. My parents made the decision that afternoon: we would all need to sleep up in the attic. I looked at the canal, where the water level was very high and the wind-swept waves grew ever darker and wilder. I was confused and worried. Would our dike behind the house break? But our house stood at the same level as the canal, so would just the pastures be flooded? As an 8-year-old, I did not understand that sea level was much higher than our canal and that a serious flooding meant our house would be at least two or three meters underwater.

My mother started organizing us all to bring supplies up to the attic. I remembered being told to carry some pillows up the 4-meter-long ladder secured to the wall in the small spare room we called the "dorsvloer" (threshing floor). I found that long ladder scary at the best of times, and bringing up a pillow or a blanket made it harder. Stepping off a ladder into the space ahead always made me uneasy.

Finding my footing going down the narrow ladder wasn't much better, but right now, someone else was hurrying me along, waiting to go up with the next load. We brought up lots of bedding supplies, food supplies, and other basics in case we'd be up there for days before being rescued. My sister Catherine recalls that Tante Lena came by to help, too.

The wind howled around the house and the rain pelted our windows. My father and the boys were in the barn tending to the animals and loosening the ropes which tied the cows down. If need be, it would now be easier to loosen the ropes entirely. Next, we all hastily ate our normal supper consisting of cheese and jam sandwiches and climbed the ladder one more time that day, my parents and nine children, aged 1 to almost 15. Our bedding was already spread out and arranged by my big sisters. A few times in the past I had been up here with an older sister to gather apple slices drying on the wooden floor, but we had never been up here as a family, together in one space.

My father gathered us in a big circle, and with a tremor in his voice, he began talking to us about what was happening. The storm was still fierce, and more dikes had broken that afternoon. We needed to pray to God to keep us safe. I squeezed my eyes shut and folded my hands tightly as my father prayed for God's mercy. He seemed like Noah to me. The wooden floor we sat on and the sloping wooden rafters under the roof were not unlike pictures of the ark I had studied in our Children's Story Bible. I remembered Noah sending out a white dove after the storm, and I noticed our attic, too, had a small window. Then it was time to go to sleep and I huddled under my blanket, feeling fear in the pit of my stomach. My mother bustled about nervously as she tried to get us all settled down. It took a long time for me to fall asleep. I woke up once, and I heard the wind still howling loudly. When I woke up again, it was morning. The wind was less loud. My father and Simon were not there – they had gone down the ladder to milk the cows. Relief washed over me.

A little later we all gathered in our normal living space to eat breakfast, and my father updated us on the storm. Many homes had been flooded, lives were lost and animals had drowned, but we were no longer in danger. Then he thanked God for sparing our lives but he prayed for all those people who had lost loved ones, their homes, their livestock. I looked outside, noticing that the water in our canal was very high, but I was reassured that the canal had stayed within its banks. Later in my life I would remember this fearful night as our one and only camping experience as a family.

A photo book consisting of black and white photographs was published that was read over and over again by people in Holland. It was called *"De Ramp"* (The Disaster) and it contained grey picture after grey picture of flooded homes, barns, people on roof tops, people in rowboats rescuing others, dead livestock, and water, water everywhere that once was land. It was the biggest natural disaster of the century for the Netherlands. In all, 1836 people drowned that weekend, 47,000 cattle and 140,000 poultry were lost, and 72,000 people were evacuated. The book was the most well-worn book we owned and it had a profound impact on us as children. It came with us to Canada.

7. SAYING GOOD-BYE

We had been spared, and for us children, life on the boerderij continued as if there had been no calamity, as if nothing had happened on the islands south of us. One lovely day that spring we once again posed happily in our orchard. Later that summer, we welcomed baby #10 to the family, Heleentje.

I am in the front row, far right.

It was the following year that our family story took a dramatic turn. After family devotions one day in June, 1954, my father asked us all to stay at the table. Solemnly he began:

"Your mother and I have something important to tell you. We are thinking about emigrating to Canada. You know that Oom Arie, Oom Wim, Tante Nan, and Tante Truus and their families all live in Canada already. Your mother and I have decided that I should go visit Canada, to see if it is a good country for us, too."

I sat in shock, open-mouthed. Dad continued, "Two weeks from now, I will fly to Canada and I will be gone for four weeks."

I was dumbfounded. My dad, going in an airplane? I didn't know if he'd ever been in a car – I myself had not ever had a ride in a car. And then to Canada? So far away? At school I had studied the map of the world. During the previous summer, my sister Tini's English teacher had started coming to our home once a week to give English lessons to my parents and the four oldest children. I had not taken much notice, because to learn English was generally a good thing. This was now getting serious. I had a lot to absorb.

The weeks my father was gone went slowly for us. Mom was anxious and we were all uneasy. Might we leave our familiar home? Our school? Our friends and our relatives? Above the gable of the front door to our home was that depiction of the two scouts returning with a cluster of grapes so big that it took two men to carry it. My father was like Joshua for me, the Biblical figure who did reconnaissance for Moses (Numbers 13). We waited eagerly, also anxiously, for my father to return from his exploratory trip.

There is a back story I was not privy to as a child. In the 1920's and 1930's, my father and his three best friends had talked regularly about emigrating to Australia, Canada, or South Africa. Their early years had been beset with Spanish Flu problems and the Great Depression, and these other countries appeared to offer more opportunities for a good life than their home country did. My father apparently told his father in 1935 that he and his fiancée wished to emigrate after their marriage. Opa was vehemently opposed, but then he offered to retire soon so that my father could take over the family farm. Which he did, in 1938. Fifteen years later my Opa died, and my father felt free to pursue his emigration dreams once again. One of his friends (Piet Keyzer) had already left for what we called "Amerika" and the other two (Uncle Harry and Roel Buinink) had gone to Canada. Pressure was mounting for my father. He now had four sons and he worried about limited opportunities for them to find farms in crowded Holland. There was also talk about expansion of the Rotterdam seaport, which might result in our polder being filled in with silt. If so, he himself would also need to find a new farm.

When my father returned from his trip to Canada, he encountered a miserable, rain-bedraggled scene. It had been very wet and cold in the previous weeks, and milking the cows in the rain-soaked, muddy pastures had been very challenging. My mother, together with the neighbour who my father had put in charge of farm operations, decided to bring the cows back into the barn, two months earlier than usual.

It did not take long for my father to make up his mind. He wanted to go to Canada. He told us that, unlike Holland, Canada was a beautiful, sunny country with plenty of opportunities for dairy farmers. My mother did not object.

She welcomed new opportunities, and she did not get along all that well with Dad's family or other Maaslanders. In addition, four of her family were already in Canada. Simon, at 16, was enthusiastic about the plan – he was already hatching his own plans to emigrate in order to avoid compulsory conscription into the Dutch army. The decision was finalized and preparations began for leaving in five months. A whole new adventure lay before us.

Formal photographs were taken for each of our passports, and so was a family portrait to mark the important occasion of our immigration (page 4). During the winter prior to our departure, I felt mostly excitement about the coming adventure. I was now also included in the family group taking English lessons, as were Corrie and Koos. At school I sensed that I had become a more important person. I had a story to tell. We were going to Canada! No one else in my class could lay claim to such fame. I felt noticed.

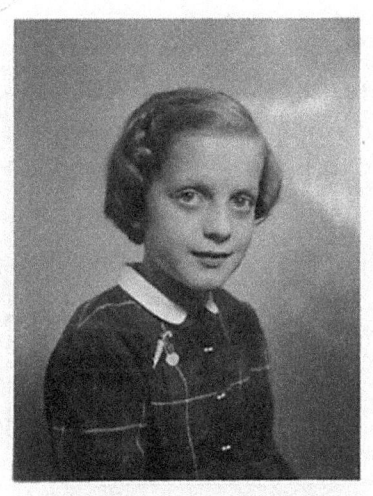

The big sea voyage was to happen in February, 1955, but a measles outbreak among the younger children in January delayed that plan. My father became very anxious because his new boss, Jim Pate, was expecting him to start as farmhand on March 1. The unusual decision was then made not to go by boat, but to fly all twelve of us to Canada in early April. Thankfully, the trip turned out to be less costly than anticipated. In the post war years, the Dutch government encouraged people to emigrate, and as of April 1, 1955, additional monies were made available for this. Our family qualified for the new subsidy, and the story has it that at the airport on April 5, my father received a very substantial sum towards our travelling costs.

For me, the day of the liquidation sale in our final week in Holland seemed like a grand party. Lots of people, lots of excitement! My big sisters were in charge of selling coffee and almond pastries, and Corrie and I assisted them. We carried plates of the pastries, offering them for a guilder a piece to the people milling about. The pastries were delicious, the best we'd ever tasted (we sampled quite a few before the day was done). After the sale was over, all of us, young and old, noticed the emptiness. Catherine recalls Mother's beautiful writing desk being sold to a neighbor, and seeing Dad's rolltop desk with its many little compartments being carried away. I remember Mom's prized new baby change table with grey marble top disappearing. She had loved it, bathed her last two babies on it. The stable was empty, too. All the cows had been shipped off a few days earlier. One of my brothers recalls the deep sadness he felt as the cows were led out of the barn. For me, the grief began after the liquidation sale. I remember feeling lost, forlorn. Our home was no longer home. I think we were all feeling sad, but we didn't speak about it to each other.

In the previous few weeks, there had been parties for saying good-bye to neighbours and relatives in my parents' panelled bedroom. I had the sense that these were emotional times, but I don't remember if there were tears shed. Until the day that we were actually leaving. I remember watching wide-eyed as many of the aunts and uncles seeing us off at the Schiphol airport became teary-eyed. They hugged each of us tightly and said sweet, caring things to us. Very unusual behaviour I had not experienced before. Many kissed us good-bye.

Before embarking on our flight, we had our photo taken. We were immortalized on the steps of another airplane, one heading to Mexico City. It was evening when

we finally departed from Schiphol. One of the memories I have of the flight itself is becoming very nauseous. A kind stewardess came over, handed me a white paper bag, and I promptly emptied the contents of my last meal into it. It was not surprising, actually. The year before I had been a backseat passenger in a Volkswagen Beetle, one of two cars loaded with family members to see my father off for his exploratory trip to Canada. It was my very first ride in a car, ever, and I became so car-sick, that the driver had to stop the car so I could vomit safely into the ditch. The same thing happened on the return trip from Amsterdam.

This time, too, my stomach was not behaving. My nausea was contagious. Soon Truus, who was seated beside me, also needed a little white bag. Our stomachs gradually settled. Then came that memorable meal served on a beautifully presented dinner tray. The stewardess told us she could not offer a tray to Truus or me, as it might get our stomachs upset again. I remember being quite hungry and disappointed, especially when the others around us started raving about how delicious the little round roasted potatoes were. Eventually we all slept a little, and thankfully, when breakfast came around, Truus and I were allowed to eat again.

THERE IS A STORY about my father and our flight across the Atlantic that has become legendary in our family. When my father returned from his reconnaissance trip the previous summer, he told us that his biggest disappointment in Canada was the quality of the potatoes. He determined that he had no choice but to bring along some seed potatoes so that we could grow better-tasting potatoes. However, sometime before our final preparations, he learned that it was illegal to bring produce into Canada. This left my father with a very serious dilemma. He was the most honest person we knew, honest to a fault sometimes, but his love of potatoes got the better of him. He told my mother to hide a few dozen of these little potatoes in the rolled-up socks in the suitcases. I remember my mother doing this last-minute task with an unhappy frown on her face. He also asked Siem to put a few in his overcoat pockets.

The story has it that my father's conscience became so uneasy during the flight over the ocean that he asked Siem to return the potatoes to him. Then he walked down the aisle towards a stewardess. Showing her these potatoes and the ones in his own pockets, he explained his contraband problem and asked her for help. She shook her head and said, "No sir, we cannot drop the potatoes out of the plane, and no, there is nothing we can do about the ones in your suitcases."

Sure enough, we ran into trouble in Montreal. When the Customs official asked my father if he had anything to declare, he confessed. The official sternly told him he'd have to hand over every one of the seed potatoes. He sent us all to another counter where Dad in turn told my mother to remove the potatoes from the suitcases.

My father telling my mother to do the deed was no surprise. He was hardly the authoritarian type, but we were accustomed to clear role definitions in our family. If Mom wasn't there serving him tea whenever he entered the kitchen, he'd order a daughter to make and serve him tea. I'm not sure if in his later years he ever did make coffee or tea. Probably no need. Similarly, my father had no experience packing or unpacking a suitcase. This particular day in the Montreal airport, I clearly remember my mother, flustered and red-faced, rummaging through all the suitcases looking for the swollen socks while a straight-faced official looked on. Mom was visibly and audibly upset with my father. It had been his idea in the first place and now she was being publicly humiliated. I'm not sure, but I think I heard her mutter angrily, "… if you had only kept your mouth shut!"

Many years later, John told me that Dad had planted the stray seed potatoes that were still found when the suitcases were unpacked. The results were disappointing. Climate and soil conditions were just not the same here as back in Holland. Happily for my father and for us, new potato strains were developed over time. Potatoes such as Yukon Golds tasted much better than the greyish, almost translucent potatoes of the 1950's.

We stopped for refuelling in Ireland and in Gander, NL. I remember shivering and seeing endless piles of snow when we briefly disembarked in Gander. Our final landing was in Montreal and from there we took a train to Toronto. My most vivid memory of our long airplane and train journey is my mother's constant and anxious counting whenever we disembarked or had to enter the plane or train again: "Do we have them all? One, two, three, four, five, six, ...," and then she'd start over again, "Mieke, help me count, one, two, three, ..."

In Toronto we were ready to take the next train to Brantford when we suddenly heard a familiar voice. Uncle Bill! Our relief when we heard his voice and saw him in the flesh was palpable. After a joyful greeting, my mother and the little ones climbed into his car and the rest of us boarded the train to finish the long journey to our new home. Our Brantford relatives were there to welcome us, but I remember very little of our arrival. I was exhausted. I fell asleep the moment my head touched the strange new pillow.

MANY YEARS LATER, I was on a quest to find out more about our emigration. During a visit to Holland in 1999, I posed the big question to a few relatives: "What did you think was the reason for Koos and Marie to leave for a distant land with so many children?" The answers varied.

Either my father was to blame, or my mother. I was expecting views attributing the big decision to my father. I was a little surprised that for some, my mother was the culprit.

Some relatives remembered our leaving well. My father had rented a small bus for our family to travel to the airport that final day in Holland, and he invited aunts and uncles from both sides of the family to join us on that bus if they wished. One of my mother's sisters on that bus told me that during the trip home from the airport, Dad's sister, Tante Lena, was very distraught. She was heard to say, "Marie? She is the one who pushed it all through!" (*"Marie? Die heeft het helemaal doorgedreven!"*)

From a cousin on Dad's side, I heard a similar sentiment. I'd offered that we had emigrated because my dad had always wanted to do that. The unexpected response: "No, the story here is that Marie dragged Koos to Canada, that she stole him from his family!" (*Het verhaal hier is dat Marie heeft Koos meegesleept naar Canada, ze heeft hem gestolen van z'n familie!*)

I was 54 years old when I learned just how big a loss it had been for my father's family when we left Holland and emigrated to Canada in 1955.

PART II

8. UNEASY TRANSITIONS

I woke up to a beautiful sunny morning. We all went outside and marvelled at our new surroundings. In the manicured lawn next to the house, we saw unfamiliar, red-breasted birds digging up worms. Beyond the lawn we noticed many striking evergreen trees and rolling hills stretching to the horizon. Hills were new to me. So were evergreen trees! They had only lived in our storybooks, in the VandeHulst children's books I had read again and again.

It did not stay peaceful and idyllic long that first day. There was so much to do! Unpacking and sorting. Meals to be made in an unfamiliar setting. Appliances and beds to be borrowed or bought. Within days, my father and Simon  were working fulltime for Mr. Pate. Before we left Holland, my father had taken driver's lessons in Rotterdam, but now he needed to obtain a driver's license and to buy our first car. Relatives and good people from the local church helped, but still! By the end of the first week, my mother was utterly frazzled and my father's face had deeper worry lines.

That first and only summer we lived on the Jim Pate farm, I remember treasuring the many warm, sunny days in Canada, so unlike Holland's rainy days. We made good use of the veranda and the vast green lawn all around the house to expand our living quarters.

Here I am, watching over the little ones on the lawn: Jack (3), Helen (2), Tommy Pate (1), Betty (5)

The little house with only two bedrooms was too small for all of us. Mattresses were placed in the narrow upstairs hallway to accommodate nine of us. To get to my bed in the girls' room, I tripped over these mattresses and tried not to be scolded by a sister for stepping on her. The living room was converted into a master bedroom, and here little Helen slept in a crib, next to Mom and Dad. With the need to find sleeping space for twelve persons, there was very little space left over for living; the eat-in kitchen served this purpose. We bumped into each other everywhere. We argued and we bickered. There were too many people, too little physical space, and too little emotional space! That pattern remained for the rest of my youth.

Our first home in Canada, on Powerline Road in Brantford

I clearly remember our first day in the one-room school. A young, friendly teacher did her best to make us feel welcome. She made flash cards to teach us classroom objects, "desk, door, window, blackboard, piano." I liked that last one, as the Dutch word for it was the same. At the end of the second day, the teacher informed us that the next day we had to go to the Tranquility School, two kilometers in the opposite direction. It was a bigger school - it had two classrooms. I was a bit sad about this news because I liked my first teacher.

Our new teacher, Mrs. Palmer, was a seasoned, take-charge person who was not fazed by having the additional assignment of teaching four new immigrants, fresh off the plane. She placed John in the grade 5-8 classroom, and Jim, Corrie and me in the grade 1-4 classroom. I remember my first Friday in Mrs. Palmer's class. Placing a piece of paper in front of me, she said, "Mieke, try the spelling dictation today."

Shaking my head, I said, "I can - not."

Firmly, she insisted I try it. I succeeded with some of the words, as Dutch is a very phonetic language. But then there was a very strange word. I wrote what I heard, which was "ve-je-dub'-bels". When I saw the correct spelling, "vegetables," I was really frustrated and muttered under my breath, "Vay-guh-tah-bless? Dat is crazy!" At home, later that day, I complained loudly that there were a lot of stupid words in the English language.

We were not prepared for the heat wave in May. We had packed lightly because we were flying, so most of our things had been shipped by sea in a *"kist"* (a very large wooden crate). We'd travelled in full winter gear because my mother had been forewarned that spring was always late in Canada. Our summer clothes were in the kist. As we slowly trudged home from school along the dusty gravel road, we found the afternoon heat unbearable. Every day our first words upon arrival home were, "Is the kist here yet?" Day after day the answer was followed by our unhappy groans.

On a cooler day that month, Corrie and I were called into Mrs. Palmer's office. We were nervous. We didn't know what was happening. The school nurse was sitting at the small table, but Mrs. Palmer stayed standing. The nurse asked us to remove our knit woolen cardigan. Then our knit woolen pullover. Next our woolen pleated skirt. Finally, our "borstrok" (knit woolen camisole) that we wore over our "hemdje" (cotton camisole). By now, we were thoroughly embarrassed. Thankfully, she let us keep on our underwear and our cotton hemdjes. Then Mrs. Palmer and the nurse explained carefully that we were dressed too warmly, that it was not healthy to wear so much warm clothing indoors. I tried to explain in my limited English that our summer clothes were still on the boat. I wanted to say, but didn't say, that my mother was not stupid, that Dutch homes were clammy and much cooler.

I really don't know why we hadn't removed our woolen cardigan when we were in the classroom. I suspect my memory about the woolen camisole is likely wrong. I wouldn't have worn that in May anymore. I do know that I found it all very humiliating, and that it was not the last time that I felt this emotion as an immigrant. Eventually the kist arrived. Summer came, and in winters to come, I avoided wearing hand-knit, woolen clothing. I had never liked itchy, scratchy, woolen garments anyway.

PRIOR TO EMIGRATING, my parents sought medical advice regarding family planning. They were 45 and 41 and already had ten children. A new pregnancy would be inconvenient as they approached this biggest adventure of their lives. For religious reasons they had always thought birth control was wrong, but they believed that the rhythm method was justified under special circumstances. The method must have worked for a while. Mom was often pregnant again around the time of a baby's first birthday, but Helen was 21 months when we arrived in Canada on April 6, 1955, and Mom was not pregnant. Not yet!

Mom was happy with her new rhythm method, but she did not realize that the severe stress of emigrating with ten children to a strange land can easily upset one's menstrual cycle and render the method useless. When Richard was conceived in early May, a month after immigration, it came as a surprise to her that this could have happened. I am quite sure Mom and Dad worried about finding space and money to care for an eleventh child, even though they assured us, their children, that they trusted in the Lord to help them.

Mom's pregnancy became special to me that fall because of an extraordinary conversation I had with her. One day, while dusting together, in a rare moment when it was just the two of us, she told me that in a couple of months we would be getting a new baby, and that it was growing inside her. I was awed. I was a naïve ten-year-old and I knew nothing about the birds and the bees. I had always thought that babies were mysteriously delivered from heaven. I used to wonder about how the doctor received the baby from heaven, how he knew where to bring the baby. Did a stork bring a little note along with the baby? Directives about where to bring the newborn? I thought doctors had an enviable position because they had the most direct contact with God. This particular day I was digesting much new information. I was also deeply moved because Mom had actually had an intimate conversation with me, and because she'd shared wonderful news with me. I was excited about this pending birth – the first one I had known about prior to the event.

I still knew nothing about how babies start growing in wombs. Years later, I would tell my mother that I did not learn about sex until grade 8, when school friends talked about it in the girls' washroom. Her response surprised me, "You didn't know? Growing up on a farm, and you didn't know?" We had been well taught at home, church, and school, that God created human beings after he created the animals, and that people were a special category. It puzzled me that she was surprised.

During the fall months it became increasingly obvious to my parents that they needed to buy their own farm soon. My father's wages and Simon's wages together, working for Mr. Pate, were only $175 per month, and even with a free house, expenses were greater than income every month. With their dwindling savings, my parents bought a 100-acre dairy farm for $23,000 in the Simcoe area. The farm on hiway 3 between Simcoe and Jarvis came with a small dairy herd and a large, five-bedroom home.

Possession date was February 1, 1956, but our moving date was delayed until after the baby's birth. My brother Simon (still only 17 years old) was sent ahead to manage the whole dairy farm on his own for a month.

Richard's birth on February 6 was the first hospital birth for my mother and not a happy one. My father was not allowed to be with her during the birth process. Hospital rules. My mother felt dreadfully alone. And misunderstood! At intake they had asked her what her maiden name was, and she had replied, "VanderKooy."

"No, what was your last name *before* you were married?"

"Ja, VanderKooy," she had answered. They repeated the question a few more times and got the same answer from my exasperated mother. They just could not comprehend that her maiden name might be the same as her married name. Her feelings of being a stupid, lower-class woman were accentuated by her lack of a comb. She had forgotten to pack one, and my father kept forgetting to bring her one.

Things were not right with the new baby. We began worrying and praying for his survival. He could not tolerate breast milk. The doctor recommended formula, then goat's milk, both to no avail. Finally, baby Ricky took to soy milk, and we were all thankful. It cost a lot, but it was well worth it if it would save his life. I recall him suffering much with eczema that first year. I worried for him. I also enjoyed watching over him. One beautiful spring day Mom had parked the baby buggy under the flowering cherry tree on the west side of the house. Ricky was gurgling and happily kicking his little feet, but then he quieted. He seemed to be listening to a song erupting from a bird in the cherry tree above him. I wondered; did I see this right? Then I saw him do it again, turning his head to listen to another bird song. I smiled happily; I was very proud of my alert little baby brother.

Our farm on Hiway 3 between Simcoe and Jarvis, in 1956.

9. SCHOOL IN CANADA

The big stories for our first year in Canada were the birth of a new baby and buying a farm, but let's back up a little to our first summer in Canada. We school children were becoming comfortable with the English language and we had acclimatized somewhat. When we arrived in Canada, we had changed our family name from "van der Kooij" to "VanderKooy." Many of us had also anglicized our first names, e.g., from Tini to Cathy, Jan to John, and Koos to Jim.

Before school started up again in September, I changed my name, too. I didn't like it when people called me "Mickey" or "Meekee," so I changed my name from Mieke to Mary.

Me, between Corrie and a new friend

More summer play dates. Back row: cousin Tena VanderKooy, Corrie, Mary. Front row: Betty, Jack, and cousin Evelyn VanderKooy.

That fall, Mrs. Palmer kept me in grade 4 so that Corrie and I could again be taught together in the grades 1-4 classroom. I found this upsetting. In Holland, the new school year started on April 1, and I had just been promoted to grade 5 when we emigrated. Adding insult to injury, Mrs. Palmer promoted Corrie to grade 4!

At home I complained bitterly about this injustice. "Why? Why is she in my grade? She belongs in grade 3! I belong in grade 5! I'm a very good student, too. This is so unfair!"

My parents just shrugged. They had no clue as to what to do about it. Six months later, when we moved to the farm between Simcoe and Jarvis, the solution came. I begged my father to make sure I would be placed in grade 5, not grade 4. He did. It helped that he could speak Dutch to the principal of the Jarvis Christian School.

The teachers and students in this school were all Dutch immigrants and members of the Christian Reformed Church. The curriculum followed provincial guidelines and was taught in English, but like in Maasland, we now had devotions at the beginning and the end of the day, and Bible was an academic subject. I noticed how much easier it was to form friendships in this school because we had so much more in common with these students than the ones in the public school in Brantford.

The Jarvis school had begun its operations six months before we arrived in the area. It was soon bursting at its seams and a third classroom was added in the summer of 1956. My teachers at this school were not notable and I did not warm up to them. A decade later I was a teacher myself and, belatedly, I acquired a measure of understanding and sympathy for my teachers. They were expected to teach a multi-grade classroom of 35-40 students with very few resources. In addition, they had also been the first two principals of this fledgling school. As such, they had an overwhelming number of additional duties and responsibilities: bus driver, teacher supervision, school discipline, curriculum and supplies decisions, board and committee meetings, parental complaints, etc.

Jarvis Christian School, with later addition

I remember being somewhat appalled by my grade 5 teacher's unseemly lunch-time behaviour, his feet up on his desk. I was particularly grossed out, but also mesmerized, by the way his large Adam's apple bobbed up and down as he chomped crudely on his sandwich. The teacher I had during the next two years also had a number of qualities and habits I found troubling. If he'd catch me doodling, he'd make an unkind remark about it. One day he spotted me drawing, half-hidden under my textbook, a picture of a pretty woman in an elegant dress. He grabbed the sketch, pinned it on the bulletin board, and mockingly said, "Mary is thinking about her wedding! Ha! Ha!" I was mortified!

I do remember that this teacher was kind to the student who had a major intellectual disability. One day this student answered a simple math question correctly, and he drew us all in to cheer for him before he rewarded him with a chocolate bar. He was less understanding towards some other students. One of my friends was not good at math and she often needed more explanation. The teacher's problem was that after our grade 6 math lesson he needed to get to the grade 7 students, and then to the grade 8 students to give instructions. He taught our group too quickly, showed only one example on the board and told us to get going. My friend would raise her hand and say she didn't know what to do. He'd shame her and say, "Oh, didn't you listen again?" Impatiently he'd repeat the lesson. This happened again and again. I would silently cringe for her and wish that I could get up to help her. But no, students were not to talk and they had to stay in their desks. In my head, I'd argue with him, "She can't help it! Don't be so hard on her!"

In retrospect, these were formative moments for me. We learn from positive experiences as well as from negative ones. Years later, I was drawn to help students like my friend, students who needed more patience, more understanding, and different learning strategies.

So why did these cash-strapped, just-off-the-boat immigrants set up Christian schools? The Jarvis school was one of many Christian schools established in Ontario by the Dutch immigrants in the 1950s and 1960s. In Holland, students from Protestant families attended Christian schools, students from Roman Catholic families attended Catholic schools, and all other students attended public schools. Following a protracted battle for educational justice and equality towards the end of the nineteenth century, all schools in Holland were state supported and funded. When the new immigrants arrived in Canada, they were very uncomfortable with the lack of educational options available to them. They felt they had no choice but to establish parent-controlled, private schools so they could be assured that the theological foundations of their children's school matched their own belief systems.

The sacrificial dedication of the parents supporting the Christian schools in those early years was admirable. Every week they sent their $5 per family tuition payment to school with their oldest child. After long days at work, many fathers spent endless hours at board and committee meetings to hammer out policy and operational decisions. To save on janitorial expenses, the mothers joined forces during spring break to deep-clean the school. My mother helped with this, too, even though she had young babies and a taxing workload at home. Many decades later, she told me that one particular time the mothers had found "Johnny," the infamous wooden chair leg used for "teaching lessons" to disobedient students. She said the mothers wanted to burn it in the stove. This was news to me! I had not realized that our mothers were less supportive of such harsh discipline than our fathers were. The mothers debated disposing of the offensive weapon, Mom told me, but they decided against it, knowing the principal would just find another stick. Corporal punishment was still a common practice in all schools at the time. In Ontario's public schools, the practice was not officially abandoned until the 1970s.

SCHOOL WAS NOT the only place we received an education. We learned many practical skills growing up on the farm. We girls learned to cook and clean, to sew and do laundry, and to soothe a crying baby. The boys learned to do barn chores, to milk the cows with electric milkers, and to do tractor and field work. In the summer, we all weeded the strawberry patch, hoed the cucumber field, and helped harvest the crops. In the haying season, I sometimes drove the tractor while stronger family members threw the hay bales on the wagon and stacked them neatly in piles.

Picking cucumbers for the pickling factory: Jim, Corrie, Betty, Mary, Helen, and my mother

In the beginning of this memoir, I unabashedly said we were born in a barn. Was this apt in an idiomatic way? The born-in-a-barn expression suggests poor manners, such as forgetting to shut the door behind you. Were we, VanderKooy children, ill-mannered? I am uncomfortable writing this, but I think the answer is: "Yes, too often! Especially in Canada!" Consideration for others was not our strong suit. We were very competitive and not good at turn-taking and sharing. We ate our food too quickly, hoping to beat others to second helpings. We excelled at interrupting and arguing at the dinner table. Putdowns and clever one-upmanship comments were all too common. I don't remember supporting or celebrating each other's troubles or successes, either.

In Holland, etiquette had been part of our training. We learned specific manners, as in, "Sit up straight, elbows off the table, don't lick your knife, say please." When an adult addressed us, it was drilled into us that we had to "answer with two words," never just one. It was to be: "Yes, uncle," not "Yes." We were taught never to touch our food with our fingers. All meals were eaten with a fork and knife, bread meals, too. Open-face sandwiches were carefully cut into small squares, then eaten with a fork. There were no hot dogs or hamburgers, and certainly no corn-on-the-cob! Corn was chicken feed!

After immigration, etiquette training and enforcement mostly went by the wayside. Dinner expectations and behaviour rules were relaxed. Mom had no more time, energy, or inclination to teach the finesses of manners. Dad? If I remember right, he'd only notice if someone outright swore.

Dad was scrupulous about no one using swear words. On rare occasions he himself was heard to use a strong Dutch expletive, such as when a cow kicked him in the shins or caused him to spill a bucket of milk, but we never heard him use words that we thought were swear words. If Dad heard someone at the farmer's co-op say, "Jesus Christ!" or "God damn," he always found it necessary to speak directly to them and say, "You may not use God's name in vain." Even to complete strangers! When I was present, I was not sure whether to be proud of him or to be embarrassed.

As children, we knew that *"vloeken"* (the Dutch word for "swearing") was a very serious offense. We knew not to use God's name in casual or disrespectful ways, so we also avoided words like "gosh" and "jeez." However, we had no problem using crude language. It took us a long time to understand that for "civilized" Canadians, some of the words we used were swear words. The crude bathroom words that rolled off our tongues so easily, words like "shit," those were words that made them cringe!

10. EVERYONE PITCHING IN

We were all relieved to have a bigger house and more living space when we moved to the farm in March 1956. With help from her older daughters, my mother got busy organizing the house. One problem she needed to solve immediately was the lack of adequate closet and storage space in our Victorian farm house. At auction sales, she found several cheap dressers for our bedrooms, but nothing that would serve as a linen cabinet in their own bedroom to store linens and their own clothes. My mother was not one to demand things for herself, but this was a need, not a want. Always resourceful, my mother found the name of a skilled Dutchman in the Calvinist Contact, a weekly newspaper for Dutch immigrants. He was able to make her a replica of the armoire she had enjoyed in Holland.

In this same paper, my mother found a Woodstock farmer who was selling all of his cheesemaking equipment. She bought it promptly, hoping that making cheese would add to our family income. In Holland, she'd successfully made Gouda-style cheese for years. At the Simcoe farm, I sometimes watched my mother work in the milking parlor next to the barn. First, she did the daily cleaning of milking pails and equipment, then she started the cheese-making process. She'd return to the milking parlor several times during the day for this. It was a tremendous amount of work: measuring, stirring, checking the temperature, straining out the whey, placing the fresh cheese in cheesecloth in wooden vats after so many days, checking some more, placing the soft round cheese wheels on clean wooden planks to cure, etc. The results were disappointing. Because humidity and other conditions were very different than in Holland, most of our cheeses turned out to be substandard. In those days there was also no demand yet for artisan cheeses. My mother wisely gave up this effort.

My father worked himself to the bone, too, during those first summers. In between milking, haying, and crop farming, he worked in tobacco to earn a few extra dollars. The older children found paying jobs to help support our family. Simon worked briefly in a chicken factory and then at the Cockshutt Farm Equipment factory. Trudy and Cathy worked in a variety of jobs, e.g., as a nanny for families, housecleaning, and farm jobs. A few years later, Simon became a mechanic and Cathy became a grocery store cashier. Between age 13 and 19, John worked fulltime on the farm with Dad.

The school children, aged ten or eleven and over, spent their summers working from early morning to dinner time to supplement the family's income. My father planted several acres of strawberries and other cash crops. My mother often joined us in the field during harvest season. I enjoyed picking the luscious strawberries in June, did not mind the hoeing in July, but in August I disliked the prickly vines of the cucumbers we picked for the pickling factory. I found the tomato harvest even more unpleasant. Moving those heavy bushels of tomatoes between the rows was exhausting.

My mother, on the right with Ricky in this photo, loved helping in the field. She'd assign me or another daughter with kitchen duty as often as possible. Here, I've just delivered hot coffee for the afternoon coffee break.

I remember one day of hoeing especially well. I think I was 13 years old. We were hoeing the new strawberry plants and Dad was motivating our little team. After coffee break, he said "Let's see who can get to the end of the row first."

Invariably, Dad was first, Corrie was a close second, I was next, and young Jim came in last. Disappointed, I determined to push myself really hard, give it my all, and beat Corrie in the next row. It didn't work. After a few more failed attempts, I made a pivotal decision. Why keep on trying to beat my sister? Doing my best at my own pace was good enough!

After a few summers, my father reduced the tomato crop because we could earn more money in the tobacco harvest. He continued planting an acre of cucumbers which he, my mother, and any children too young to work in tobacco could still manage.

During my high school years, I worked in tobacco alongside Corrie, John, and later also Jim. Starting in early August, the tobacco farmers on the other side of Simcoe needed large crews to pick the leaves, string them on sticks, and hang them in kilns to be cured. If my memory serves me well, our earnings ranged from $11 to $14 per day. We did the work with little complaint. The first hour of tobacco work could be unpleasant, as the wet-with-dew leaves soaked us to the bone, but mostly it was a positive work and social experience.

Our first boss lady introduced us to pizza (home-made) for lunch. The following year we worked for the Bakker family and we all boarded at their home during the week. Every morning Mrs. Bakker prepared a delicious breakfast of eggs, bacon, and fried potatoes for her family and crew. Compared to the toast and tea breakfast at home, this was royal treatment. We worked alongside some teen boys we knew from church connections and they added an exciting dimension to our work experience. Their transistor radio introduced us to upbeat, contemporary music not heard in our home. Corrie and I still hum "An itsy bitsy teenie weenie yellow polka dot bikini ..." when we recall those summers in tobacco.

Being able to contribute to the family's financial resources instilled a feeling of pride is us. We did not keep any of the money we earned in tobacco, but at the end of the summer, Dad gave us a little money as reward. One summer he was particularly generous, giving us $10 each. I loved having some money in the tin can serving as my piggy bank, and I dreamed for weeks about how I would spend it. I settled on buying each of my eleven siblings something for Sinterklaas on Dec. 5 (Dutch Santa Claus tradition), and I puzzled long and hard about suitable gifts that would fall within my budget. Then, late fall, another cow died and there were worries that milk production was below quota, a serious problem which could result in losing quota! Dad very politely came to each of us, asking if we could donate from our piggy bank to help him buy a cow. I felt quite grown up being asked to do this, and I very happily opened my piggy bank and handed him the $10. I would not be able to give St. Nick's gifts, but I was content that my money had gone for a more urgent cause. I think I suppressed the feeling of relief that I no longer had to solve the puzzle of buying so many gifts with my tiny stash!

Life was not all work and no play during these years. We did not quarrel all the time, either. Sometimes we enjoyed playing board games or doing jigsaw puzzles together on a Sunday afternoon. In the summer, we often piled into the cab or into the back of our pick-up truck after the day's field work was done. We drove a mile down the highway to the deep quarry, then eagerly jumped into its cool waters. We had no shower at home, and this clean-up was faster and much more fun. We never saw other people swim here, and we thought of the quarry as our own.

With Corrie and my father

Sometimes we played in the hay barn. When we had friends over, they loved playing in the hay, too. We'd climb up the ladder to get to the top of the mountain of hay bales, then play tag or re-arrange the bales to make tunnels and mazes. I always hoped John or Corrie wouldn't get it into their heads to walk across the beam to get to the other side of the barn, where loose hay was piled high. Once there, they'd compete to see how far they could jump into the hay pile. The narrow beam we had to traverse was at least four meters above the hay barn floor. Even as a child, my balance was not good. I tried crossing the beam once. It terrified me so much that I never attempted it again. When they changed the game, I had no choice but to go down the ladder and wander off by myself.

The second summer on the farm I had a nightmarish accident during haying season. Using the tractor, my father had pulled a wagonload of haybales up the steep ramp into the hay barn, which was directly above the cow barn. John and Dad emptied the wagon and now the wagon had to be brought down. Dad attached a thick rope to the wagon hitch and asked any young children nearby to help pull on the rope to slow the wagon's descent down the ramp. I was near the tail end of the rope which Dad had placed around one of the barn posts. Dad manually pushed the wagon towards the edge of the haybarn, then began steering and pulling really hard on the arm to restrain the wagon as it rapidly picked up speed. We all pulled on the rope to assist. Suddenly the rope behind me fishtailed, wrapped itself around my left leg, and yanked me off my feet. My leg smacked against the post and I was dragged downhill behind the wagon at great speed, screaming at the top of my lungs all the while. I did not let go of the rope until the wagon stopped.

I continued screaming! The pain above my left ankle was fierce. Dad came running towards me, looking very worried. He asked if I could stand on my leg. I couldn't, and I kept wailing. He then picked me up and carried me gently to the sofa in the front parlor. When my pain had not subsided after several hours, my father drove me to the hospital. An X-ray determined that my leg was indeed broken. I remember Dr. McGavin, our family doctor, talking to the nurse as together they made a plaster cast for my injured leg. "These immigrants! Using their young children for farm work! It's just terrible!"

They continued discussing immigrants as if I was not there. I found their talk really upsetting. I said nothing, but I wanted to say, "I hear you. I understand English! My Dad didn't make me help him, I volunteered. It's not his fault! It was just an accident!"

On crutches at Niagara Falls in 1957, with my father and Corrie.

11. MY TEENAGE YEARS

I remember feeling nervous, a little lost, those first days and weeks in high school in 1958. The Simcoe Composite School was huge! It had 1600 students, and 13 classes for just grade nine students. I had come from a three-room school where all the students were Dutch immigrants. Gradually, I learned to navigate the school halls, the schedules, and teacher expectations. I loved the school library and having access to a wealth of books.

Eating lunch in the high school cafeteria was a novelty. The cafeteria smelled wonderfully of food freshly cooked, and I looked with some envy at the kids lining up at the counter every day to buy a full, hot lunch. Most students ate home-made lunches, although many lined up afterwards for fries or a dessert. Our family's financial resources were still very meagre, so I was careful not to ask my mother for money unless it was absolutely necessary. Some mornings I asked her for a dime. Then I, too, lined up at the lunch counter. With my dime, I could buy a bowl of warm soup or a carton of milk. I'd agonize about the decision. Soup would be really nice, but milk was healthy and would help me swallow my dry sandwiches. I think soup won out more often. I didn't ask for another dime for at least another month or more. I knew my mother would give me one if I asked, but I worried that she really couldn't spare the dime.

As a family, we managed to spend very little on clothing during these first years in Canada. Our own hand-me-downs were supplemented by clothing we received from other sources. Quite a few times, the old dominee of the Jarvis church drove up our long driveway bearing gifts. As he unloaded his car, he explained that he'd received another shipment from the churches in Grand Rapids, Michigan, and he knew our large family would be happy to receive the donations. We sure were. We'd all quickly look through the boxes hoping to lay claim to the best items.

I learned to sew my own clothes once I was in high school. I signed up for home economics classes for four years, against the advice of my guidance counsellor, as these courses were typically designed for students less academically inclined. I loved the sewing and foods classes, so I persuaded her

that someday I might want to teach Home Economics. At that time, it was cheaper to make your own clothes rather than buy them off the rack in the store. It was well before Canada started importing cheap clothing from countries like China. I liked being able to select my own patterns and fabrics. I remember making a tailored blue wool suit with lining and interlining in my grade 12 sewing class. It felt like a real accomplishment.

In my later teen years, I was still supplementing my wardrobe with donated clothing. I know, because in one box of donations, I found the smart-looking outfit and a necklace to complement it for my first day of school in grade 13. That was the year that our family was featured in the local paper because eight of us were starting school. My "freebie" outfit was immortalized on the front page of *The Simcoe Reformer* (Sept. 2, 1962).

This family photo, also published in this local paper, included all but Simon, who was married and living in Toronto. Baby Caroline is 3 months old here.

AS A STUDENT raised in the Reformed theological tradition, high school came with some personal dilemmas. One day in grade 9, the Physical Education teacher announced that at the beginning of next month we would start our dance unit. I heard her announcement with consternation and some panic. I didn't know how to dance! In my family there was little or no appreciation for rhythm and physical movement, and the thought of being able to move gracefully seemed an impossibility.

Worse, there was a strong prohibition against dancing in our tradition. Christian young people did not dance, as dancing could lead to sex. In my small town of Maasland, no one danced. The closest people got to dancing was playing a game of musical chairs at a celebration or festivity. They also did not play games with classic card decks - those could lead to gambling. They did, however, enjoy "memory" and other card games. Movies? There was no movie theatre in Maasland, so it was easy in our small town to keep young people away from the worldly temptations espoused in movies. In nearby Dutch cities, the culture was changing and many church people there were becoming more relaxed about moral constraints.

I took my dilemma about dancing in class to my mother. She ended up writing a note for my teacher in which she requested an exemption for me from this unit. Much later, I would wonder how she knew to write this note, or who helped her write it.

I do remember those two weeks of P. E. well. There I stood, off to the side in the big gymnasium, all by myself. Watching the other students move to music, some more awkwardly than others, but all having a good time. In grade 10, I stood off to the side again, still exempted from the dance unit. By this time, I was experiencing some mental turmoil. The classes looked like fun, and I was starting to question the church taboo against dancing. Why had I told my mother about this unit? She would never have known. By grade 11, I had strong regrets, wishing that I was participating in the class rather than standing conspicuously to the side. I did not ask my teacher to let me be included now. What would I say? It's no longer against my religion?

Another unsettling experience happened in a geography class. Mr. Lemery taught this class. I knew him well. After we moved to the farm, my father had hired him for quite some months to tutor my parents and the older children at home. My parents liked him, and found him to be a good teacher of English language skills. He also taught us basic knowledge of Canada, which was important for passing the Canadian citizenship exam, which we did in 1960. So, in the beginning of my grade 10 geography class, I felt at ease. I knew Mr. Lemery, and I trusted him. That changed a month later, when he started teaching a unit on the origin of the Earth. His lessons were wholly opposed to what I had been taught. If I remember right, he taught us the theory of continental drift, and also its recent update, the theory of plate tectonics. I was deeply troubled. Was Mr. Lemery not a member of one of the mainline churches in Simcoe? How could he teach that the earth was millions of years old, that it was shifting and changing? I was very uncomfortable in his next classes. I'd lost respect for him. He had upset and shaken my stable worldview.

THE CHURCH PLAYED a big role in our lives. My father dedicated many hours of his time to church work. He was an elder and also the first clerk of council for the new

Simcoe Christian Reformed Church. This meant he was away at evening meetings at least twice a week, attending a council meeting or doing a family visit with another elder. When he was home on other evenings, he was often at his small desk in the front parlor, writing the minutes for the church meetings. Cigar smoke curled up lazily from the cigar in his left hand, creating a light gray haze around him. To this day, the scent of a good cigar brings a peaceful, tranquil image to my mind: my father, writing and smoking in the front parlor, my mother in the dining room, sitting quietly, folding laundry or darning a sock.

It was a relief for my father when in 1960 Rev. John Vriend arrived to become the church's first pastor and take over some of the responsibilities of the elders. I did a lot of babysitting for the Vriend family that first year. Mrs. Vriend had a soft-spoken, gentle manner and I cherished the way she treated me with respect. I was delighted when she invited me to come along for their family vacation at a cottage in northern Michigan the next summer. While helping to take care of their five children, I got to hang out with "rich people." It was a novel experience! I even tried water skiing, unsuccessfully.

Mrs. Vriend, a teacher prior to her marriage, was a wise mentor and role model for me. One day I talked to her about my predicament, that I was not sure whether to become a fashion designer or a teacher. (I had just designed the cover page for the fashion show hosted by my grade 12 Home

Economics class.) Mrs. Vriend thought for a moment, then gently told me that as a teacher, she had often wished that she could draw better, to help explain things for her students. What an astute woman! My career path became clear to me at that moment.

Memorable was the trip which Rev. Vriend organized for our young people in 1962. We visited Grand Rapids and Holland, Michigan, to become acquainted with the roots of the Christian Reformed Church. For an immigrant teen like me, the cultural exposure was more notable than the history lessons about our church. I was awed by my hosts. With their perfect manners, placemats and napkins, and unfamiliar breakfast foods, like halved grapefruit and yoghurt, they seemed so cultured!

All of us were impressed with the lunch buffet in the cafeteria at Calvin College. It offered an abundance of delicious looking foods, including peaches and what we thought was whipped cream. One fellow in our group eagerly served himself a full bowl of the latter. He shovelled a huge spoonful of the "cream" into his mouth, only to unceremoniously spit it out all over the cafeteria floor the next moment. It was his and our introduction to cottage cheese.

One of my friends in the Simcoe high school attended the local Baptist church, and sometimes we debated the merits of infant baptism versus adult baptism. I tried to persuade her that infant baptism was correct, that our church had it right. With time, I became less sure of myself. In my final year at home, I attended a very small Profession of Faith class – just me and Magda Dreyer. I posed the troubling baptism issue to Rev. Vriend. I give him credit for not just giving me a simple, rote answer, the way my church elders had done. He had me read various expert materials and we explored the historical context for the varying views. In the end, we came to the conclusion that there might not be a single right answer, and that these doctrinal differences were not all that important to the basic question of faith. I came to understand that I was born into a Dutch Reformed family and with that came certain traditions and viewpoints.

Me, Rev. J. Vriend, and Magda Dreyer

During my early teens, I liked spending Sundays with my friend Magda. The Dreyer family lived in an old brick home on Norfolk Street in Simcoe. Town offered more excitement than our farm, even if in those days all the stores were closed for Sunday observance. If I'd suggest we go for a walk downtown, Magda was always a good sport. The main game was to attract whistles from young guys cruising by in shiny new convertibles or rusty old jalopies. Truth be told, we weren't all that successful at this game. If occasionally some guys drove by and did whistle at us, we were thrilled and we'd giggle all the way home.

I'd always bring along a book to read, and we spent hours reading up in Magda's bedroom. Magda's mother told me she liked having me over. I think she liked that we read books. I liked being in their home, too. Magda was the oldest of eight children, and her parents were interesting. Her father was a fun-loving, talkative, and jovial sort of man. Her mother was a kind, gentle soul who showed a genuine interest in me.

I especially enjoyed dinner times at their home. Magda's parents engaged me in their table talk, conversing with me as if I was an adult. Her mother loved serious topics, like, "Do you think it is right, Mary, that your father lets his children skate on your pond on Sunday afternoons? As an elder, should he not set a better example? My children are not allowed to skate because at the arena they have to pay a fee and cause people to have to work on the sabbath day."

I loved the dialogue, and I fervently defended my father's actions. Magda's father had a more humorous bent. I remember him saying one Sunday, "Hey Mary, isn't this a great dinner?" Steak, mashed potatoes, green beans and apple sauce were Sunday dinner staples. As he took another bite from his T-bone steak, he continued, "All those farmers with big bank loans aren't eating like this!" He rubbed his rounding belly with delight. Sunday dessert was invariably instant vanilla pudding and whipped cream at their home. Magda and her mother would clear the table for dessert while her father happily showed off his expertise at whipping the cream until stiff peaks formed.

One particular Sunday, he asked with a big grin on his face, "Hey look, Mary, you know how you can tell that the cream has been whipped long enough? If you hold the bowl upside down and it doesn't fall out, it's done." As he said this, he poised the bowl full of whipped cream over my head and turned it over. The unthinkable happened. All the cream slid smoothly out of the bowl and plopped on my head. Gobs of the white stuff cascaded down my face, my neck, the back of my head. First there was a momentary silence around me, then shrieks and gales of laughter. The loudest laughter came from Magda's father.

I was in shock, not sure whether to laugh or cry. Evening church was in one hour, and how could I go to church looking like this? Magda's mother chuckled and cooed, "Oh dear, dear, let's clean you up." Magda, too, made sympathetic noises, but she couldn't stop laughing. Her mother helped wipe the worst of the gooey mess off my face and hair before sending me and Magda to the bathroom with a clean washcloth and hand towel. I washed my face, but my hair was hopeless. Washing my hair was not a possibility. There were no hairdryers yet, and walking into church with wet hair was never done. My greasy locks looked like I'd applied a half tube of Brylcream, like I had a really bad Elvis hairdo.

Magda's mother suggested that I stay home from church and ask my family to pick me up after evening church. I called my dad. I explained my problem and nervously begged him to allow me to stay home from church. His answer was swift: "No, you go to church!"

My tears flowed in earnest now, from frustration and embarrassment. Magda tried to reassure me, that my hair didn't look so bad. I remember little about the actual church experience. I do remember that I was angry at my dad for being so rigid, for causing me this humiliation and mortification. I was also really angry at myself. Why, oh why had I called him to ask for permission? Magda's parents would have had no problem explaining why I needed to be picked up at their house after church. In future years, I'd be less inclined to ask my father for things that might result in an undesired response.

12. MY MOTHER AND I

I frequently butted heads with my mother during my teens. Unlike some of my sisters, who were more restrained in expression of their feelings, I was vocal and argumentative. Sometimes it was about food. I had an intense dislike for some of the simple fare we ate, and I wanted to cook some new foods I was learning about in my home economics classes at school. I especially disliked the white rice we ate on Saturdays, cooked in milk with raisins and served with melted butter and cinnamon sugar. It was our main course, followed by a milky dessert such as a thin oatmeal porridge cooked in milk, or a thin cooked custard. I thought rice served this way was revolting. Once we started buying ketchup, a Canadian staple, I removed the raisins and added ketchup to my rice. Only slightly less disgusting.

To stop my complaining, Mom offered to let me cook dinner one Saturday. I suggested a recipe that included onions, but she said, "No, Dad does not like onions." Then I asked to make one of several rice dishes that included tomatoes. The answer was no again, for the same reason. I became exasperated and loudly I proclaimed, "I will never marry a man who does not like onions or tomatoes!" (Luckily for me, Adrian loved both!)

Our disputes over food continued. To my mother's credit, she wisely finished one of these arguments with, "Someday I'd like to have a meal in your house!" It was a hopeful comment, but the emphasis was on "someday." Right now, she was in charge.

Another source of our conflict was about decorating for Christmas and setting a festive table. Christmas at our home was indistinguishable from a regular Sunday. I wanted to have candles in the centre of the table. Mom objected, "Your dad does not like candles. He wants to see what he is eating."

Evergreen boughs were nixed as well, and I gave my mother a hard time about this, too. Little did I know at the time that she had some sympathy for my wanting to create a more festive, Christmas atmosphere. In our protestant church tradition, icons and ornamentation were discouraged because it distracted from the real Biblical message. After WWII, however, Christmas trees and festive lights were becoming increasingly popular in Dutch cities. Not so much yet in small towns. My father liked things simple and he resisted any changes, so nothing doing in our house. Catherine recalls that when she was little, it happened one Christmas day that Mom prepared the supper table and placed a large red handkerchief over a wall lamp, instantly creating a soft red glow in the room. The children were delighted! Mom hoped my father would not object too much when he came in from milking the cows. Alas, before he entered the house, the red handkerchief caught fire! That was the end of decorating for Christmas. For a while. By the time I was grown and had left the house, Christmas trees, candles, and roast turkey dinners had become a regular part of our family's celebrations. A television had also made its entrance into our family home.

In my mid-teens, Mom was often frustrated with me for not cleaning up my room well enough. I shared this bedroom with two or three sisters, but I was the oldest. Truth be told, I was sentimental about things and probably had the most "mess" in our room. One day Mom was so exasperated with me, she told Dad to give me a tongue-lashing. He took me to my bedroom and admonished me for not listening to my mother and tidying up as I'd been told. He finished his lecture with a warning, "If you do not learn how to keep your room neat, no one will want to marry you!"

When I wanted to go to some event, I had to ask my mother for permission. Often the answer was negative. When I'd get really frustrated with her for thwarting my desires again, I'd head to the barn, hoping to have my father speak sense into her. While I complained, he listened quietly, then he'd say, "Your mother has decided. You listen to your mother." He never offered to talk to her on my behalf, or told me he understood my frustration. If I carried on complaining about Mom, his refrain was, "Your mother has many good qualities."

Sometimes I'd continue with "You are both so unfair! Everybody else can go!" His answer was invariably, "We won't let you because we love you!" After parenting my own children, I am a little more sympathetic. Sometimes loving discipline does require parents to say no to their children. At the time, I remember muttering angrily to myself as I walked away from the barn, "The only time I hear that you love me is when you refuse me something I want!"

My mother loved babies and little ones, but she was less affectionate and comfortable with children over four. They didn't always cooperate and they developed minds of their own. And parenting teenagers? This age group certainly catapulted my mother out of her comfort zone. And to say that she was ambivalent about sexuality would be an understatement. If our task as daughters was to attract a future husband, she gave us no helpful guidance or encouragement. She just worried about things going wrong.

If I stopped to look in a mirror to adjust some stray hairs, I was warned not to be vain. One day, perhaps in grade 10, I walked into the kitchen wearing lipstick. With a disapproving look, my mother said, "That is what whores do, too!" Her comment bothered me, but it didn't stop me from wearing lipstick, doing what my peers were doing. She said no more about it. My grade 10 school photo shows I have begun using lipstick and touching up my eyebrows.

In my teens, our social life consisted of Sunday church services, Catechism, and Young People's. Most interesting were the regional Young Peoples meetings in Hamilton. These monthly Saturday evenings were wholesome events consisting of prayers, Bible reading, a message by a pastor, and hymn singing. The excitement was being with so many girls and boys from other churches, looking over the boys, and hoping to attract the attention of at least one of them. My mother understood this and was often reluctant to give me permission to go. One time, her answer was very graphic: "No! Definitely not! *De beste koeien worden op stal verkocht.*" (The best cows are sold in the home barn.)

I was not happy to be compared to a cow, but I had read enough Jane Austen novels by this time to understand her drift. Walking off in an angry huff, I yelled back at her, "I haven't seen any buyers or gentlemen come calling here!"

My first date was awful, a bad memory! A week before the August Civic holiday, a boy I had met in Hamilton and will call Henry, phoned to invite me to go to the Elora Choir Festival with him. Very hesitantly my mother gave permission. An hour later she changed her mind. She said that at 16, I was too young. She ordered me to call Henry to cancel the date. I thought that was rude and I refused. Mom got even with me. On the important day, she made me join the cucumber-picking crew at 7:00 a.m. and she wouldn't let me stop until 10:00 am, the exact time Henry was to pick me up. My anger at my mother when I finally came out of the cucumber patch, all dusty and dirty in my field clothing, changed to deep embarrassment when I met Henry in the farmyard and I had to ask him for a little more time to clean up. In the Elora Park, young people strolled from choir event to choir event, or they just took in the sights. Many walked in pairs, holding hands. Henry tried that, too, but I kept finding reasons to drop his hand. The worst part of the day came at the end. The moment Henry drove up our long driveway and reached our house, my mother came charging out of the house towards him. Puzzled, he lowered his window and she began berating him angrily for returning her young daughter at such a late hour. (It was only 8:30 pm and it was still light out.) I burst into tears, jumped out of the car, and ran into the house. Poor Henry! It was my first and only date with him.

SATURDAYS WERE NOT my favourite days when I was in my teens. Mom assigned us a ton of housework. Dusting, wiping, polishing, cleaning the toilet, and washing floors. One of my regular chores was polishing at least 20 pairs of leather shoes which I lined up on newspaper on the kitchen table. While a great workout for my biceps, the shoes likely heard a lot of unhappy muttering. Besides washing floors downstairs, there was all the dusting and dry mopping to be done in the four bedrooms upstairs. Doing upstairs was the worst task on my list.

Why did the sneezing always start on Saturdays? I never made the connection. We had no knowledge of allergies, let alone dust allergies, and our family doctor ignored me when I complained that I had a "perpetual cold." Not until I was 18 and started having severe outbreaks of hives and full-blown asthma did this doctor finally suggest that I had "allergies" and that I should see a specialist.

In the meantime, even I wondered why I was feeling so irritable, arguing so much with my sisters and snapping at little and big brothers. I'd spend the rest of the weekend sneezing and looking for more clean handkerchiefs for my poor, sore nose. On Sundays, the days I most wanted to look good, my sneezing continued almost non-stop!

My mother was a hard task master. She'd check if Corrie and I had adequately dusted all furniture, baseboards, stairs, etc., and if she was not satisfied, she'd make us do it again. The list was long and I would try to work faster, hoping to have a little more time to do homework, to sketch, or to read my novel. To no avail. If I told Mom I was finished, she'd find me a new job to do.

One day, late in her life, my mother told me a story about her childhood which caused me to totally reframe my perspective on my own childhood. She told me how little time she'd been given to play. When she and her sisters came home for lunch for an hour on school days, they had defined chores to do, like setting the table and knitting a set number of rows on their socks. After school there were more regular chores and additional tasks assigned by their mother.

"There was no play time," said my mother. "I'd hear neighbourhood children playing on the street. I'd look out the window and see my friends having fun skipping, or playing marbles, and I'd feel so envious. I decided, then and there, that I would never do this to my children."

I think my jaw dropped as she said this. I was close to 50, and not until this moment had I realized that my mother had given me, us, plenty of play time! On weekdays I'd always had free time after school, and our only tasks were setting the dinner table and doing the dinner dishes. I'd never noticed. On Sundays, chores were religiously kept to a minimum. Saturdays were workdays, but even then, later in the afternoon I again had free time. And in Holland, before I turned 10? I have no memory of having to work at anything. Just play time! My dear mother had kept her word!

13. NIGHTMARE

If you asked me what was the most difficult part of my childhood, I would answer without hesitation: my illnesses and losing my sister. It is time to tell these stories.

Trudy and I both had a history of serious illnesses. When we were little and there was a measles or chicken pox outbreak in the family, we were more ill than the others, my mother told me. This was corroborated by my father's comments in the family letters which he contributed to regularly in the 1940s and 1950s.

I vividly remember the first time that I thought I was dying. I was five years old and I was experiencing powerful cramping in my tummy. I knew that pain in the tummy meant imminent death. How was I so sure? Years later I learned that my Tante Bep died of ovarian cancer when I was five, and that the fatal symptom was pain in her belly. This particular night, as I lay curled up in my bed in fetal position, the discomfort became worse, and I did the unthinkable. I got out of bed and went to my mother. In between sobs I told her: "*Ik ga dood!*" (I am dying). As I anticipated, she gave me a stern scolding for getting out of bed, and with an unsympathetic, Dutch version of "Don't be silly!" she sent me right back to bed. For years I remembered this experience as an example of my mother's insensitive ways. A kinder interpretation might be that her matter-of-factness provided me with reassurance that I would be fine. True, but my mother's manner that evening showed that comforting and providing emotional support to her children was not her forte.

Moving to Canada in 1955 was a seismic shift for our family. So far, I have described some of the ways our first years after immigration were marked by general stress and intense family efforts to earn a few extra dollars. I haven't told the half of it yet! It was family illness that really marked these years. My own debilitating illnesses frequently overwhelmed me, but it was Trudy's illness that most profoundly impacted me and our whole family.

In November, 1956, an outbreak of mumps kept me and six others in bed for a while. I don't remember much about it, except that my neck was painfully swollen. Catherine remembers that she did not become ill and that she felt like Florence Nightingale as she helped to care for all the sick children in the four bedrooms upstairs.

Five months later, in March, 1957, I became very fatigued and the whites of my eyes and my skin turned an ochre yellow colour. I was diagnosed with hepatitis A. My younger brother, Jack, also became ill with what we called "*geelzucht.*" Treatment was lots of bedrest and sucking on hard raspberry candies. I liked the candy part, but have always wondered about this part of the treatment. Did Dr. McGavin really give my mother this advice, and was it one more example of his questionable medical knowledge and practices? Or was my mother feeling badly for us and consoling us in her own tried-and-true ways? I know that I spent much time in bed, and that I missed school for six weeks. I must still have done well enough in school, because in June, my teacher/principal promoted me directly from grade 6 to grade 8.

That summer, I suffered the farm accident in which I broke my leg. Then, in the fall of 1957, just six months after our family's hepatitis outbreak, the Asian flu (H2N2) pandemic struck the world and our family. I don't remember how many in the family became ill. I just know that I became critically ill with this flu, suffering complications of double pneumonia and pleurisy. I was coughing up bloodied phlegm by the cupful and every breath I took felt like a knife going through my left side. I was still very ill when we received an obituary notice from the Netherlands. We opened the notice and learned shocking news. My cousin Ria, also age 12, had just died of this very same flu! I talked to no one about my heightened fears, that I, too, might die.

A few years later, in grade 11, I was seriously ill again. Within a day or two, a head cold became a serious chest cold. This time it also became pneumonia. Illness meant missing school, and this always caused me much anxiety. How would I get my work caught up, and how would I pass tests and exams, let alone do well on them? I was a very conscientious student and I studied too hard during exam times. I often studied until midnight and had Dad wake me when he got up for barn chores, at 5:00 am. Then I studied a few more hours before the school bus came. It is quite telling that it was in the middle of November exams that I became ill with pneumonia. Four months later, during March exams, it happened again. This time, Dr. McGavin had me hospitalized. It was my third bout of pneumonia. I missed 65 school days during this difficult school year. This is also the year that I missed my sister Trudy. She was very ill, but not at home. That is a story I will soon tell.

Being a sickly child was not something I enjoyed, as one of my siblings once surmised. Admittedly, I did get more attention from Mom during these times. I recall that when I was very ill, she sometimes came upstairs with a bowl of specially-made, delicious tomato soup and a small Gouda cheese sandwich to eat in bed. She'd sit on the edge of my bed and gently ask me how I was feeling. If I looked a little improved, she'd encourage me to come down for my next meal.

After I had eaten a few lunches downstairs, Mom would ask: "Do you think you feel well enough to stay up for a while?"

I now have a confession to make. I read a lot of books while I was sick. Only when I was very ill, did I not read. I had to hide my reading, because if Mom knew that I was reading in bed, she'd figure I was well enough to be put to work. Therefore, when she asked me that question, I recognized a trap.

"Oh, no!" I sometimes whimpered in a tired sounding voice, "I'm exhausted from being up just fifteen minutes!" Mom let me be, and I made a convincing show of dragging myself back to bed. Once there, I guiltily continued reading my book, blankets pulled high to hide my surreptitious activity.

In my teens, I experienced life as precarious. Before I was 21, I would suffer from more pneumonias and respiratory illnesses, severe, undiagnosed allergies, and asthma. I would never really understand what people meant by the phrase, "Youth feels invincible."

I DO NOT REMEMBER when the nightmare started. I think it was a few years after we immigrated. It continued for years. The dream was always the same. I would be waiting nervously with my bike for the Maasluis ferry. The bike inexplicably disappeared before my dream was over. There were many other people, also waiting for the ferry. The sky was dark and ominous. The fog horn sounded and the ferry came into view. With a loud clang the ferry hit the dock wall and was secured by ferry workers. As the ramp came down, everyone around me started pushing and shoving to get on first. My anxiety escalated to a feeling of panic as I inched forward. I remember feeling very worried that the ferry would pull away before I was able to get on. I almost stepped onto the ramp when, with a sudden tug, the ferry lurched forward, and the tiny gap between the wall and boat instantly grew very wide! Down, down, down, I fell! In freefall, towards the frighteningly dark, churning waters!

I would wake up with a jolt at this point, sweating profusely and thoroughly frightened. It would take a while for me to realize with relief that I was fine and in my own bed, and to begin breathing normally again.

I was still having these nightmares after Adrian and I were married in 1966. We compared notes on our nightmares and the verbalizing helped. It seemed my dreams began when stress levels in my life and in the life of my family were escalating. I was always on my way to my Opa when I fell into the abyss. My Opa, whom I was fond of, and who represented simple childhood happiness and security for me.

My nightmare seemed to signify a basic loss of security. Why was this? I used to think that my dream symbolized that immigration had caused me to lose my footing. I no longer think so. It's true that immigration had stopped being an adventure. The first few years had been interesting years. I had learned to speak a new language, become familiar with people in a different culture in Brantford, moved to the farm in Simcoe, and made new friends at school. Transitioning to the Simcoe high school was not easy, as I was still shy and lacking in confidence about Canadian ways, but it, too, was manageable for me.

No, what really destabilized me, what caused me to lose my equilibrium, was my ill health! I was so sick, and so often. I worried about dying. I worried that planning for my future was a futile exercise. Would I make it to my twenties? Whenever I was sick, I prayed fervently for healing, but I knew that God does not always answer prayers the way we would like. Sadly, I had no one to talk to about my fears.

In the meantime, my parents were overwhelmed with trying to make their way in a strange new country, with financial worries, more babies, and serious illness in the family. They had lost their footing, too!

14. TRUDY BECOMES ILL

Trudy was five years older than me and for a while she was my role model. She was very capable, an ideal oldest daughter in a large family. She had all the virtues my mother looked for in daughters: helpful, obedient, a quick study, an organizer, a good housekeeper, and good with babies. Like my mother, if my memory is correct, she also tended to impatience and a sharp tongue whenever someone in the family messed up a newly washed floor. I shared some of those attributes with Trudy, though not all of them. I was more likely to escape from household chores to my favourite pastimes of reading, drawing, or just dreaming happily in my own private world.

The first time Trudy was in a hospital, she was just 4. She had bronchitis. A few years later, Trudy nearly died because the village doctor failed to diagnose acute appendicitis. When her appendix ruptured, she was critically ill for some time in the Delft hospital.

When my brother Jack and I became ill with hepatitis in 1957, my mother was careful about contagion. She ordered Jack and me to use our own designated hand towel, not the family one hanging on a hook beside the kitchen sink. My mother almost succeeded in containing the illness. Trudy started feeling unwell around this time. In a letter to Oom Teun on April 5, 1957, Dad wrote "The hepatitis patients are doing better …… Trudy is '*oververmoeid*' (overtired)." Trudy did not turn yellow as we had. Her illness went undetected for a long time.

Trudy was working as a nanny for a family in Hamilton at the time, and she seemed to be dragging her feet more and more when she returned home on weekends. Mom became increasingly concerned and sent her to our family doctor for a check-up. Dr. McGavin surmised that she was suffering from normal hormonal issues. He did no follow-up work. That fall, my parents asked Trudy to quit her job in Hamilton so that she could get more rest and also help mom as she was able. Her condition worsened. Mom sent her back to the doctor. He again shrugged his shoulders, saying that he was not sure why Trudy was so lethargic and exhausted. Perhaps he thought she was depressed. Again, he failed to order a single blood or urine sample test. Mom and Dad were worried.

The answer to what ailed Trudy came in an unexpected way. During the winter months we did not go to the outhouse if we had to pee during the night. We had several chamber pots upstairs for this purpose. Trudy and I shared a small walk-in closet at the top of the stairs, and in this closet Trudy had her own pot. One wintry morning in 1958, while I was rummaging through this closet looking for a skirt to wear, I was startled by what I saw in her pot. Her urine was bright orange, bright like an orange peel! I hurried to get Mom, saying, "Come upstairs, please. I think I know what might be wrong with Trudy!" Mom followed me upstairs. As I pointed to the chamber pot, I told her, "When I was sick with '*geelzucht*' last year, my urine was that colour, too!" I'll never forget my mother's shocked face and her response, "*Meid, toch!* That's not right!" Mom took action right away. She sent Trudy off to the doctor with a urine sample.

This time Dr. McGavin did take notice. Preliminary tests determined that Trudy did indeed have hepatitis. Months later, she was sent to the hospital in London where further tests showed that she had advanced liver disease. My parents were told that her illness was incurable and terminal, but that they were not to tell her that as she would lose hope. They followed the doctor's orders, unquestioningly. Much later, my mother told me that this decision caused her much pain and regret. At the time, we children knew only that Trudy was ill.

WHEN WE MOVED from Brantford to the farm between Jarvis and Simcoe in 1956, we found the plumbing to be primitive, as primitive as in our previous home. There was a small hand pump beside the kitchen sink which drew water from the dug well on the east side of the house. It was mighty hard work to pump enough water for all the needs in our big household, so within a year, Dad hired a plumber to install a simple pressure system that allowed us to just turn on a tap to get water from that well. It was still just cold water, and Mom still had to heat many pans of water for doing all the laundry in the basement every Monday morning, but it was an improvement.

That dug well turned out to be a problem for our family. I learned the full story from my brother John not so long ago. He had quit school in the spring of 1957 and was dad's right-hand man until he returned to school five years later to get his high school education. As John remembers it, one day in 1957 my mother complained to Dad about the smell of our drinking water, so he and Dad set out to investigate the source. The well on the sandy hill near the kitchen was covered by a wooden platform on which was perched a pump. The  platform was in a pretty advanced stage of decay. They lifted the pump, then removed the platform. The well was about a meter in diameter. Armed with a flashlight, they looked down into the dark well, and were shocked to see several large rats in various states of decay floating on the water's surface. John recalls that they said very little to each other. He thinks Dad did not tell Mom about what they found and probably ordered her to stay away. They proceeded to empty the well of everything and then poured a bottle of chlorine down the well. The next day they emptied the well again and repeated the process. Then Dad called our handyman who sealed the collar of the well and made a cover of poured concrete to complete the job. There would be no more animals falling into that well. John noted that he and dad never talked about this event again, but that they probably should have. This contaminated well was the likely source of our family's hepatitis outbreak.

Why was the tainted well not talked about? I do not recall any conversation about the cause of our hepatitis outbreak. Some illnesses just happened, were not preventable at the time, like measles or mumps. When any of us got sick, we just prayed for healing and did not question why. That was my childhood impression, but apparently the adults did think about it. Thirty years later, my mother mentioned that she'd always been quite sure that the contaminated well was the cause of Trudy's illness and death, but that my father would not talk about it with her. John's more recent story confirmed her theory. Was it just too painful for our parents to talk about? Did my father have deep regret, wishing that he had attended to that broken platform the first time he'd noticed it? And my mother, was she trying hard not to blame my father after the fact for this terrible oversight? Our parents, who were overwhelmed with the insane busy-ness and pressures of trying to make a living in a new country? They would not have been the first grieving parents who found themselves unable to talk about their immense pain and many regrets.

TRUDY'S LONG ILLNESS was marked by up and down periods. There were times when she was so ill that she spent much time in bed. Other times she had a little more energy and was a bit more involved in the day-to-day affairs of our busy family. There was much going on. We had plenty of laying chickens now, and Corrie and I candled their eggs in the dark basement, looking for defects or bloody spots.

This was during the time that my mother was also making cheese. On Saturdays, Dad took a few of us young children (Mary, Corrie, Jim, Betty) into town to go door to door selling farm fresh eggs and wedges of Dutch cheese. Dad chose more well-to-do neighbourhoods for this. We trotted up to the doors of our regular customers first, then made cold calls until our baskets were empty. I remember we sometimes made not-so-nice comments to each other if a customer bought only a half dozen eggs, like, "How come these rich people are so stingy?"

As a younger sister, it didn't register on me that Trudy's life must have been very boring. At times Trudy did get cabin fever. On one particular Saturday that spring in 1959, she asked to go to town with us. She wanted to visit a family where she had worked as a nanny a while back. As Dad dropped her off, Trudy offered to walk to a specific corner in town after her visit and wait for us to pick her up. We carried on to sell our farm products. When we finally arrived at the pick-up point, we found Trudy doubled over on a bench, clutching her stomach and wailing. We could tell by the way she was crying that she was in extreme pain. Dad helped her gently and awkwardly into the front seat of our car. That whole trip home we were very quiet, afraid for our big sister. My mother knew what to do. She called the doctor, who came to the house and decided that Trudy needed to be admitted to the hospital. Again! Test results showed that Trudy had torn an abdominal ligament and suffered serious damage to her liver. It was many days before Trudy's health stabilized enough for her to leave the hospital to return home to us. My mother forever regretted that she had allowed Trudy to go on this trip, that she had not stopped her from wearing her fancy high-heeled shoes that day, and that my father had made her walk so far.

Family Photo, 1959: Trudy far left, my mother with Canadian-born little ones, Ricky and Peter. Only Simon is missing.

It was 1959, and Trudy had been seriously ill for more than a year now. Winter would come again soon. The doctor expressed concern about the lack of heat and lack of bathroom facilities in our old farmhouse. There was a wood stove in the kitchen which kept that space warm during cold days. In the dining room there was a small oil stove. Its pipe vented through a bedroom upstairs and then through the chimney, but it did little to heat the rest of the house. The front room (parlour), the hall and staircase, and the bedrooms upstairs were all very cold on wintry days. Water on a bedside table didn't quite freeze, but almost. Trudy had the bedroom with the stovepipe running through it, making that room marginally warmer. More alarming to the doctor was the lack of proper toilet facilities for this sick patient.

By this time I was 14, and going to the *WC* (Dutch acronym for toilet, which stands for Water Closet and was pronounced as "way-say") several times per day was always an unpleasant necessity. The five-bedroom farmhouse was the third house I'd now lived in, and its outhouse was primitive and foul-smelling. I can't say that the toilet facilities in our previous houses had been any better.

In my first home, the historic boerderij in Holland, our toilet was halfway down the cow stable. I hated having to go, because I had to pass a dozen rear ends of cows before reaching the door to the WC. I feared that just as I was coming by, a cow would lift its tail to do its business. It happened frequently enough for my fears to be real. I'd try to lean away from the gutter on my left, but hugging the wall on my right was equally foul, as it was filthy with flies and manure splatters. So, I prayed for a clear path to the toilet. And back. The toilet itself was a proper white porcelain toilet, but it had no flush. It was perched over a deep hole. No hand washing facilities either. Thinking back on this WC, its redeeming feature was its warmth, as the cows in the stable generated lots of humid heat.

In my second home, the one on Jim Pate's farm in Brantford, there was a real outhouse. It was one of those which would later be romanticized by some people who had never had to use one, or be painted by artists who loved old fences and broken-down barns as their subjects. The outhouse at Pate's farm was primitive, bitterly cold in winter, and fly-infested during summers. It was not a place to linger.

The outhouse at our Simcoe farmhouse was a slight improvement. It was a back shed attached to the mudroom of the house. On the right side of this narrow little room was a pile of chopped wood for feeding the wood stove in the kitchen. On the left side were primitive toilet facilities - a rough plank at seat height with a round hole in its center.

Under the plank was a five-gallon pail ready to catch our wastes. Small squares of newspaper were skewered onto a nail nearby and served as toilet paper. Ripping up newspaper to make enough squares for a week's supply was one of the Saturday chores for the younger children. Our red brick farmhouse had been well enough constructed for its day (early 20th century), but this back shed was a poorly-executed afterthought. Its walls were made of recycled old barn boards and were far from airtight. On snowy, windy days a layer of snow covered the toilet seat plank, and on such days, we always grabbed a coat off one of the dozen hooks in the mudroom before going to the WC.

After listening to the doctor's concerns, Dad knew he had no choice but to find funds for renovations somewhere, somehow. He was over-extended at the bank, as he had bought more cows and farm equipment to improve the farm's productivity. He went begging. He asked one of Trudy's previous employers for a loan, and they graciously obliged.

Before long, major improvements were made to the old farm house. An oil furnace was installed in the basement. Ducts were added to provide more even heating on the main floor of the house. Some of this warm air travelled upstairs, making the bedrooms a little less chilly in winter. The plumber came again, this time to install a hot water heater and to add more water lines. Because there would be increased demand, water under pressure was brought from the much deeper well in the middle of the farm yard. This well was already used for the cows and all the barn chores. Unfortunately, this water had a strong sulphuric base, so when we turned on a tap, a foul, rotten egg smell wafted up to our noses. Sometimes a guest pulled a funny face after taking their first and only sip of our tap water. The water was fine for most everything, but for drinking and cooking purposes, we continued to fetch water from the other well.

One of the small rooms off the dining room was converted to a bathroom, and this was the improvement we children cherished the most. Not only did it house a fine flush toilet, but it also had a sink and a reclaimed clawfoot bathtub. Mom cleverly asked the carpenter to make a little trapdoor behind the tub so that we could drop soiled laundry straight down to her washing machine area. We felt a little guilty about getting all these new luxuries, knowing that if Trudy had not been so ill, the changes would not have been made. She suffered, and we benefitted. However, we soon suppressed any uncomfortable feelings. We now had a bathroom, and the word WC dropped from our vocabulary. We started having a new problem, though, and that was a regular line-up for a turn in the bathroom, some just wriggling and squirming, others knocking impatiently on the door and yelling, "Hurry up! I have to pee!"

Our house had become more livable and comfortable, but Trudy's health did not improve. She continued to be very fatigued and suffered much with very itchy skin. The corticosteroids she took for her skin problems led to side effects such as weight gain, puffiness, and discoloured skin. It made her less attractive and sad. She was now 20 years old, socially isolated, and lonely. Everyone in the family was busy with their own activities. Simon and Catherine had their jobs, John helped Dad on the farm, six of us attended school every day, and Mom had two little ones at home and ran her busy household. Trudy had good friends in Holland, but she'd had little opportunity to cultivate strong new friendships since arriving in Canada. Before her illness she had enjoyed some church events, such as those hosted by

Young Peoples, but she could no longer participate in those activities.

It pains me that I remember so little from this time in my sister's life. Like others, I took her for granted. When  Trudy was not well, we hardly noticed her. Or was it that we felt helpless, that we didn't know what to do for her? Whenever she felt a little better, she'd help Mom with household chores, and then she could sometimes be quite irritable. When Trudy left the room to go to her bed, I would sometimes see Mom watch her go, and sigh deeply. Sometimes Trudy would go away for a little "holiday," spending a few days or a week with a kind relative, like Tante Rie in Cayuga.

OUR DUTCH RELATIVES knew that Trudy was seriously ill and that she was homesick for the old country. In the spring of 1960, Opa (my mother's father) offered to pay Trudy's airfare if she wanted to come for a long visit. Mom and Dad acquiesced reluctantly. Opa believed that medical care was better in the Netherlands, and if he hired Trudy as his "housekeeper," she would be fully covered by his insurance, should she need medical care. At home, medical and pharmaceutical costs for Trudy's care were high. In Canada, it was not until 1966 that universal public health care became available.

I only vaguely remember Trudy's departure sometime that spring. Her initial letters to us were upbeat. She loved being back in her old home country and spending time with Opa and visiting old friends and many uncles and aunts. A few months later, Trudy suffered a relapse. She was admitted to Eudokia, a general hospital in Rotterdam. (Prior to World War II, Eudokia was a Christian hospital for the chronically ill.) There, Trudy went from bad to worse. In her letters, she tried to stay positive. She didn't let on about the extent of her suffering.

Trudy was a patient for more than a year in that hospital. It was a terrible time for Mom and Dad, having a very ill daughter so far, far away. Dad prayed for her at every meal and Mom sighed deeply after reading one of Trudy's letters or a letter from one of her sisters in which they wrote about visiting Trudy. We were all very worried. I missed my sister! I couldn't talk to her on a phone because no one had personal phones in those days and because long distance

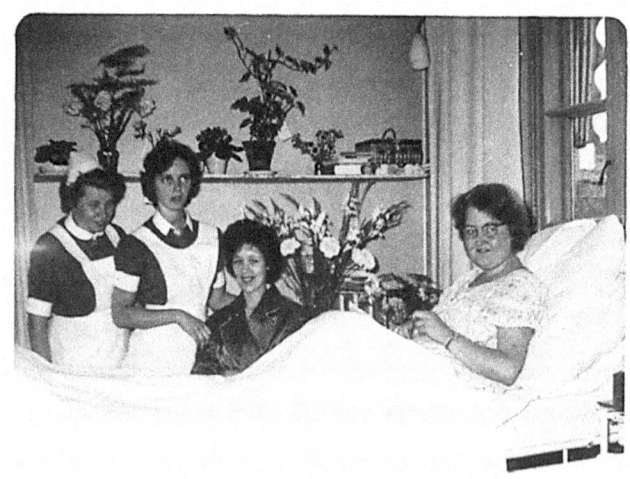

calls to the hospital were much too expensive and for emergencies only.

I felt guilt-ridden because I didn't write many letters to Trudy. And what was I going to write about? My biology class in school? Conversations I was having with my school bus friend? That I was worried about term tests coming up? I might have asked her what a typical day looked like for her, or told her about the cute antics of our youngest brothers, Ricky and Peter. But this is adult hindsight talking. I know that I found it hard to write letters to my sister. Our worlds were miles and miles apart!

It was a full 18 months before Trudy was able to return to us. Mom and Dad had started begging Tante Aaf, Mom's oldest sister, and Oom Huib to find a way to extricate Trudy from the hospital. This took some doing because medical treatments in Eudokia had turned out to be less advanced than we had hoped. Trudy had been given full bedrest, based on an outdated belief that a sick person heals faster if they do not move, do not expend energy. No walks down the hall, not even to the bathroom! That's what we learned in early letters! I have always wondered about the no-walks-to-the-bathroom part. Was Trudy's bed in an old section? Were the washrooms too far away? Did they have her use a commode, instead? What we know for sure is that after her prolonged stay in the hospital, Trudy could barely walk. After she was released, Tante Aaf took care of Trudy for several weeks at their home. This was to rehabilitate her a little before she could attempt the big journey home.

If my memory of her departure is vague, my memory of Trudy's homecoming in the fall of 1961 remains crystal clear. Dad was picking her up at the Toronto airport. I was standing in the dining room, near the doorway to the back hall leading to the stairs up to the bedrooms. I heard the car coming up the gravel driveway, car doors opening. I waited. Trudy was greeted first by people in the kitchen, then she made her way into the dining room where the rest of us were waiting. I watched in horror as she moved very slowly and carefully, hanging on to doorposts and furniture for support. My sister could not walk! And she didn't look the same! She seemed bloated, and her face was all puffy and blotchy. Then, as she greeted her brothers and sisters in the room, one by one, very formally, she sounded different! Her voice seemed to be an octave higher and she had a new, citified accent. She no longer spoke our language, the Maasland's dialect. It was then that I lost control. Before she got to me, I turned away and ran upstairs to my bed. Under my blankets I sobbed and sobbed for the sister I'd lost.

Later that day I spent time with Trudy, greeting her properly and getting to know her again. Trudy's return was very emotional for all of us. Mom and Dad were more than relieved to finally have their sick daughter home! Gradually, we all adjusted to being together again.

15. MORE BABIES

After my brother Richard was born, Mom and Dad gave up on the rhythm method. Besides, at age 43, my mother's worries about future pregnancies would soon be over, she thought. Not yet, as it turned out. I don't remember much about Mom's pregnancy with Peter. It must have been easier. We now lived in a spacious, five-bedroom house on our own farm, and we had made the initial adjustment to life in Canada. Peter was born in February 1958, around the time that Trudy was becoming more and more ill.

While Trudy was in the Rotterdam hospital in 1960, Mom became worried about her own health. It was early fall and she hadn't been feeling well. One Sunday morning she found that she could no longer fit into the skirt of her maroon suit, the suit she had first worn in Holland. Mom made an appointment with Dr. McGavin.

In a heavy Dutch accent, she said, "Dokter, I am worried ... I think I have a tumour."

He listened to her concerns, examined her, and then said, "No. You are pregnant, about three months pregnant."

Mom was surprised that this was happening again. She was 46. Absorbing the news, she carried on with her chores and the big project she had begun the previous week, repainting the kitchen. I was 15 at this time and she no longer kept news like this secret from me. A week later the cramping started and she suffered her third miscarriage. The first two had happened during the war years. If I remember right, she took this loss in stride, trusting that God knew best. Until new information came her way. She learned that pregnant women should not do any painting because of lead toxicity in paints. Not only that, it was the kitchen she had repainted, the place where she spent most of her waking hours, so she'd had much exposure to the toxic fumes. It really troubled her that her actions might have caused the miscarriage. I remember trying to reassure her, telling her that she did not know, that she should not feel so responsible.

My mother's last pregnancy is a special story. In the fall of 1961, my mother again missed her menstrual periods. She assumed that she was now really in the menopause. Again, she noticed that she no longer fit into her best skirt, and became worried. Again, the doctor reassured her, "No, it is not a tumour. You are carrying a baby."

I remember the day towards the end of 1961 when our parents told us all that they were expecting another baby, their thirteenth. I remember it especially well because two of my older siblings, John and Trudy, hurled strong accusations at Mom and Dad for doing this to all of us. John made his feelings plain, that they shouldn't be doing this anymore at their age. Trudy's reaction scared me more. She was very upset. Sobbing, she grabbed her coat and rushed outside. I watched through the window as she made her way towards the barnyard, climbed over the gates and continued, stumbling a little along the way. She headed further, down the lane that stretched between our fields towards the railroad tracks and beyond. I could no longer see her, and I worried. She was gone for many hours. Dad searched for her by car and he finally found her, in a total state of exhaustion. She had walked to the railroad track, then headed east towards the gravel sideroad, and continued further on the back roads.

The next day, I asked Trudy what was going on, why was she not happy about the new baby. She explained what was troubling her so deeply, and what she had told Dad after he picked her up: "You have no time for the children you have now! No time to give them the attention they need! What were you thinking!!!"

I was confused. I had felt excitement when I first heard a new baby was coming. Mom had smiled when Dad announced it, and he seemed happy, too. Babies were always welcomed into our family as a gift from God. When those two voices dissented, I was mystified. I was only 16, and I had not given much thought to the idea that people have choices, that they don't have to make babies, that children have the right to love and affection, that parents have an obligation to their existing children. Trudy had raised new thoughts in my mind. Did other people have lives that were less chaotic and crazy busy? Did they do things to manage their lives better? We had always felt special because we were the largest family we knew, but I had not thought about these implications. Trudy had touched on the dark underbelly of our large family.

In Mom's later years, I asked her once how she felt about it when she discovered that she was pregnant again, with number seven, or eight, or whatever number. Her answer:

"Well, at first I was not happy about it, and I'd think, "Oh no, not already! Then after a while, the idea of a new baby would grow on me, especially once I could feel the baby move inside me, that's always so special. Gradually, I'd become excited about the birth of the new baby." A typical answer for mom, as you could always count on her to be frank and real.

That is how it was in early 1962 for us as a family, too. Life went on. Excitement built. No one criticized my parents anymore. In fact, we thought it was quite neat to make the record book. One of our own making. We were pretty special in our own eyes. Our parents were having a baby when their combined ages, 48 and 52, would be 100!

THE IMMEDIATE EXCITEMENT was the first wedding in the family. Simon and Ina were to get married in Toronto in late May, but since Mom was due in early June, the engaged couple was persuaded to get married in April, so that Mom could attend.

I remember shopping with Mom for fabric for the maternity top she wanted to make for the wedding. She chose a cotton print - a small pink and green floral pattern on white background. I thought it was very plain and wanted her to select something a little more elegant, but as per usual, she had little patience for checking out options. "No, let's just pick this one."

Mom happily wore her maternity top and a black skirt as mother of the groom. I remember feeling slightly embarrassed by her shape and her outfit, but the feeling was mixed with a sense of pride. My mother held her head high. She wore the same outfit for their 25th wedding anniversary celebration a week later.

My parents celebrated their 25th wedding anniversary on May 4, 1962. Ina was now part of the family, and Caroline will soon make her entrance.

On a Sunday morning in early June, Mom went into labour. As the contractions picked up, she asked dad to bring her to the hospital. She was nervous, as she still did not like the way babies were delivered in Canada. In Holland, babies were delivered at home, the midwife assisting through the stages of labour. Sometimes the doctor was there, too. Here in Canada, home delivery was never done, and fathers were not permitted in hospital labour and delivery rooms. With her previous Canadian births, she had felt very alone and not respected by nursing staff. This time she did not fare much better. By Sunday evening, labour had subsided and they sent her home. She was embarrassed, thinking those nurses must be wondering how, after having twelve children, she still could not recognize real labour!

The following Saturday evening, Mom's contractions resumed, seriously this time. On Sunday morning, June 10, 1962, Dad arrived home with a huge smile on his face, announcing happily, "We have a new baby girl!"

We were elated and asked excitedly, "What's her name?"

"Well," Dad answered, "you can help with that. What name would you like to give her? I like Louise for a middle name, but you can pick her first name."

We could not believe our ears. You mean we'd actually get to choose her name? All the other names in the family had followed a traditional pattern. The first son was named after the father's father, the second one after the mother's father, etc. As third daughter, I was named Maria, after my mother. For good measure, I was given a middle name, Elizabeth, after Tante Bep, who was single. Twelve names, and each name had a logical explanation. For the thirteenth, my parents were throwing tradition out the window!

We spent the rest of Sunday coming up with a host of names, then short listing, until finally agreeing on "Caroline" as our favourite name. I have no idea if it was just the girls who spent the day happily thinking about names, or if some of the boys were also involved. I'm quite sure Dad took our suggestion to Mom in the hospital for final approval. So, Caroline Louise it was. This act of involving us in choosing her name was brilliant. In many ways, she became "our baby." And Trudy's baby, too.

Christmas, 1962: Caroline, eager to join the dinner table crowd.

Mom with first grandchild Jim on her lap, and Dad with daughter Caroline, who is baby Jim's aunt and only six months older than her nephew.

16. THE DOMINEE'S VISIT

Trudy was ill in the bedroom across the hall from mine, and I was lying in my own bedroom, sick with bronchitis. Just a few weeks ago I had started grade 13. This was not a good year to miss school, but I was sick enough to surrender to the prescribed rest cure, nervous that I might become ill with pneumonia again. That illness frightened me. In most of the novels I had read, characters became ill with pneumonia and died. I'd already had several bouts of pneumonia - would the next one be the end of me? Much later, it occurred to me that the books with the dreaded deaths were all written before the invention of penicillin. At the time, however, my fears seemed well-grounded. I worried that I might not see the age of 21. I hoped and prayed that I would.

Today I was worried about Trudy. Our church's pastor was visiting her this morning. I felt apprehensive about this visit. Trudy was ill, extremely ill. I knew that. Recently she had spent another week in the Simcoe hospital for more tests. But why was the dominee coming today? This

September day in 1962? Something about the visit seemed unusual, seemed amiss. I did not know that the doctor had shared the results of the latest hospital tests with my parents, and then had somberly told them that Trudy would not be long. It was time to tell her. I can only guess how my parents came to the decision to call the dominee, Rev. Vriend. Was that a typical role for the spiritual leader of the flock? Or was it just too hard for them to tell her themselves?

I remember clearly that Trudy was expecting Rev. Vriend at 10:00 am that morning. I heard his car coming up the driveway. I heard sounds of voices as he greeted my parents in the kitchen. I heard him come up the stairs and greet Trudy solemnly. I remember that the visit happened behind a closed door. I could not hear their conversation. I don't remember how long he was there. Then, her bedroom door opened, and I heard his heavy footsteps descending slowly down the stairs. Moments later, Trudy came running into my room, sobbing like I'd never heard her sob before, "I don't want to die! ….. I don't want to die! ….. I don't want to die!"

Trying to come up for air in between sobs, she told me what Rev. Vriend had told her. She would soon die. Likely within the next four weeks. She continued to sob, heartrending sobs. I remember my shock. I didn't know what to say! I don't remember if I said anything at all. I think I tried to console her, but I don't know how. I do remember feeling a deep sense of personal relief: it could have been me. I had been spared, this time. The dominee had not come to visit my room to give me a death sentence. I do know for sure that I knew enough to keep these guilty thoughts to myself.

WE WERE VERY upset about Trudy's prognosis. I'm not sure how we communicated that, if we did. Actually, I don't think we all knew. I do remember that Trudy became angry, fighting the notion that the end was near for her. Miraculously, she recovered. Four weeks later she was up and about, spending much less time in her bed upstairs. She helped with the family chores and helped with care of the little ones. Often, she'd be on the flimsy lounge chair in the warmer dining room, carefully embroidering floral patterns on table cloths and making fine cross-stitch pictures. She was part of the family again. My father added a prayer of thanksgiving to our mealtime prayers.

One of Trudy's fine needlepoints

Caroline was a smiling and responsive baby. There were lots of people to engage with her in our big family, but Trudy was a favourite for Caroline. She was not hurrying off anywhere, and on her cot in the dining room, she was closer to her eye level. Caroline liked to pull herself up to standing position at Trudy's cot and then babble and chat with her. In her final few weeks, Trudy started to come to terms with the end being near. One day, while having a sweet conversation with baby Caroline, Trudy turned to Mom who was folding laundry nearby, and said, "I know why you got baby Caroline, it was so that you would be comforted when I am gone." Mom dropped the diaper she was folding, totally caught off guard. Then she shook her head and waved with her hand as if to communicate, "Let's not talk about that." It was a missed opportunity, and Mom knew she should pick it up again. One day she would confide in me that it was one of her many regrets, that she had talked so little with Trudy about things that really mattered.

A month after the Dominee's visit, the Simcoe CRC joined other local churches to prepare for the Leighton Ford crusade coming to the little town of Simcoe in February 1963. Leighton Ford was an evangelist who conducted smaller crusades similar to the crusades conducted by his famous brother-in-law, Billy Graham. Trudy's improved health allowed her to join Catherine, Corrie and me at special preparatory meetings that fall and winter. Trudy was thrilled to be well enough to participate in the actual crusade, and afterwards to follow up with some of the people who came forward during the altar call.

But then, in late March, Trudy became ill with the flu and she grew increasingly weary. Her colour became more jaundiced and her stomach was severely distended. She spent much time in bed. Although we didn't know it, she was aware that the end was near. I'm not sure exactly when and to whom, but I know she said, "It is all right now. I am ready to die. God has given me an extra half year. He gave me the opportunity to serve him. I am ready now."

17. LOSING OUR SISTER

Trudy needed to be admitted to the hospital again, we learned when we came home from school that Thursday in late April. She was severely ill. Dad would take her when he was finished milking that evening.

Trudy was lying on her cot in the dining room, and she seemed nervous and upset. She asked me to get her the things she'd need for the hospital. It was not much - a nightie, a toothbrush, toothpaste, and a comb. Irritably, she told me to get the other comb. She fretted about her messy, oily hair. She had been too sick to wash it for quite a while, and it desperately needed washing, at least in her mind. As she was much too weak to wash it herself, I offered to help her. She got up carefully from her cot, and I supported her as she shuffled to the bathroom. She sat on the chair I placed in front of the small sink, and I leaned over her to wet her curly red hair. I worked the shampoo in, and then with a small beaker I began to rinse her hair. I remember clearly the grey and green floor tiles under our feet, the old claw foot tub behind us.

Trudy was so tired, so weak, and so unhappy. So anxious and apprehensive. But we did not talk about those things. I remember it was not an easy task, rinsing the shampoo out of her hair. It hurt her to bend over the small sink, but I needed to keep rinsing until the water in the sink was clear. I worried about her pain and discomfort, but I was trying to do a good job for her. Next, I towel-dried her hair. Was I rough? Rougher than I needed to be? I'm not sure. I do know that she was in pain and could not tolerate much.

Now, it was time to comb her hair and to finger shape her naturally curly hair. She told me what to do, and I tried to follow her instructions. She was not happy. I was not getting it right. I tried harder, but I was still not getting the curls and waves positioned the way she wanted them. Frustrated, she snapped at me, and I snapped back that I was doing the best I could. Actually, I'm not sure what I said, but I don't think it was kind. I relived this scene many times in my head. Did I hand her the comb and say irritably, "Do it yourself, then"? Or was it some other insensitive line? I do know I felt badly that I had not been able to make her happy about her hair. For many years, I deeply regretted not being kinder and more patient with my poor, dear, dying sister as I washed her hair that final time.

I don't remember if and how I said goodbye to her before she left for the hospital, or if any of the others lined up to wish her well. I know we didn't give her a hug; we never gave hugs. The hair washing turned out to be the last interaction Trudy and I had together. It was not what I expected. She had always returned home from her hospital stays.

I do not recall any family talk about Trudy being so ill that she would die soon. Mom and Dad visited Trudy every evening after milking and chores were done. I'm not sure if they made any extra visits during these last days, or if they took any of the children along to the hospital. I remember asking them after they returned from their visits how Trudy was doing, and that their news was never good, always worrisome. Trudy was very, very sick.

I did not visit Trudy in the hospital. I don't know why I didn't go, why I did not ask to go visit her. Was it my job to babysit, to put the little ones to bed? Likely that was the reason I didn't go those last evenings, as the next oldest girl at home was Betty, and she was only twelve at the time. As far as I remember, the boys did not babysit because they did farm chores. But why did I not ask to go visit on my own, during the day, like on Saturday when I was not in school? I was 18 and I'd had my driver's license for more than a year. Surely the family car was not in use every hour of the day. This question has long troubled and puzzled me. It fits with the pattern. While mature and capable in some ways, in other ways I always took direction from others. I took little initiative to identify or pursue my own desires. For example, I never asked for the car to go to the library or to a special school event. That would have seemed frivolous, wasteful of gas money. I only drove the car occasionally, and that was when dad wanted me to drive mom somewhere because he was too busy with other things. John usually did the driving for church events, such as catechism. I worried about Trudy, I thought about her a lot, but I did not visit her those last days that she was in the hospital.

IT WAS TUESDAY evening. Trudy had been in the hospital since Thursday evening. Mom and Dad returned from their evening visit at about 8:30 pm and busied themselves doing a few final evening chores. Dad wrote a letter at his small desk in the front parlor before retiring for the night. Mom put away a few piles of folded laundry and set the table for breakfast, then turned in, too. When the telephone rang, I had finished my homework and was reading a novel in my bed. Betty and Helen were sound asleep in the small bed next to mine. I looked at my alarm clock: it was 11:00 pm. This was very late for a phone call.

With a sense of foreboding, I climbed out of bed and kneeled down at the top of the stairs to listen. Who was calling at this hour? I could hear my mother answer the phone, then after a minute, say, "*Ja, dokter,* ..." and I knew in the pit of my stomach that there was really bad news. I tiptoed down the stairs and stood anxiously behind the slightly ajar hallway door, listening to my mother's answers to the doctor. She sounded terribly upset, and forgetting the English she knew, she answered the doctor in Dutch, " *Ja dokter,* ... *Ja, we kommen gelijk.*" (We are coming right away.)

After Mom hung up the phone, I opened the door wider, and noticed that Dad had come out of bed, too. Mom placed her hands over her face, and trying to control her voice, told us what the doctor had said. Trudy had taken a turn for the worse after they had left ... she was vomiting blood ... she was dying. I began to cry. Dad looked very, very sad, and Mom started to cry, "Oh Trudy, Trudy, ..."

They pulled themselves together and started to think about what had to be done. First, they called Rev. Vriend to let him know about the doctor's phone call. They told me to call the children living away from home, Simon, Cathy, and Corrie, to tell them what was happening. Then they left for the hospital.

I returned to my bedroom to find some socks to wear, and I noticed Betty was awake. I shared the very sad news with her. Then telling her to go back to sleep, I went downstairs again. I had a task to do. First, I called Simon and gave him the news. I called Cathy next, and she surprised me with her decisive, unusual response. She said she was going to step in her car to go directly to the Simcoe hospital. Lastly, I called Corrie. She had been serving as a mother's helper for a family in St. Catharines since January. She was only 16 and unlike Catherine, she had no car. Corrie asked me what she should do, how quickly she should come home, and I had no idea. I might have blurted something like, "There is nothing you can do, so no hurry necessary." How wrong I was. We might have cried together. We might have consoled each other. We might have been company for each other.

As it was, there were many of us spending this terrible night alone. Once I had done my tasks, I wandered aimlessly around the house, not knowing what to do, constantly thinking about Trudy in the hospital. I desperately wanted to be there, too, to touch her lovingly, to say something nice to her, just one more time. I knew that could not happen. There was no other car. I was responsible for the eight little ones and not so little ones sleeping in this house. Mom called from the hospital and gave me an update. I told her about the calls I had made. I had a job to do. I needed to take care of things here at home!

I went back to bed, but sleep would not come. I was in shock! The worst thing imaginable was happening. My sister was dying. I cried softly, but I wanted to howl. I wanted to wake the rest of them to tell them that Trudy was dying, to cry and to wail together, but I was sensible and responsible, and I reminded myself that they needed their sleep, there was nothing they could do.

Years later, Elizabeth (Betty) told me how she had not been able to sleep anymore, either, and was quietly dealing with her own grief. When I experienced the deaths of our parents in the 1990's, I finally understood what I was missing that horrific night in 1963. It was an adult to hug me, to hold me, to comfort me. I was a child, we were all still children, left alone with a terrible burden. We had no one to make a cup of tea for us, to sit with us, the way caring people did for us when our parents died. I could only imagine how lonely Corrie must have felt the night Trudy died. She did not dare tell the VanderMaas family that she needed to go home. I had given her no encouragement. And Simon, what was it like for him? Trudy was only sixteen months younger, and they had grown up together.

Eventually I dozed off on the couch in the front parlor. I woke when I heard Dad in the kitchen. It was 6:00 am. Anxious for more news, I got up to talk to him. He told me that Trudy was semi-conscious when he'd left her in the middle of the night to get some sleep before milking the cows. Cathy and Mom had gone to Rev. Vriend's house to stay near the hospital. Dad was about ready to head out to the barn when the phone rang again. It was a hospital nurse, calling to say that Trudy had asked for her mother and father. After telling John he would have to start milking alone, Dad drove off to pick Mom up at Rev. Vriend's house and then to head to the hospital.

About an hour and a half later, Dad and Mom returned. With a lump in my throat, I noted their red-rimmed, tear-swollen eyes. They told us it would be very soon now. Trudy had given a beautiful testimony of her faith, and she was no longer conscious. Then Dad went to the barn, and Mom headed to the kitchen to attend to things there. We took our cues from them, and we got busy, too.

No one went to school that day. The house was quieter than usual – there was no playfulness and no bickering among the school-aged children. I disappeared to the bedroom I shared with Betty and Helen at night, trying in vain to focus on a homework assignment. Just before ten o'clock, the phone rang again, and I ran down the stairs to listen in. Others had also been drawn to the dining room by the phone ringing on the wall. Dad had just come in from the barn for coffee time, and he took the call. It was Rev. Vriend, calling from the hospital, telling us that Trudy had died at 9:45 am and that she had died calmly and peacefully. Some started to cry, others turned away quietly and disappeared. Dad spoke to the ones who remained in the room. He said Trudy was in heaven now, in a better place. Mom tearfully nodded her head. I just remember a searing pain in the pit of my stomach.

18. THE FUNERAL

After the initial shock, things got really busy. In addition to regular chores and activities, there were so many things to arrange. We didn't have to deal with feelings if we kept busy. We'd been raised to keep some feelings private. We could show unhappiness through irritability or angry outbursts, but feelings of sadness, confusion, or fear were not readily expressed. Life was about survival, about doing things that needed immediate attention.

Simon and Corrie had to be called again. Arrangements had to be made with the funeral home. Announcements were crafted, a telegram was sent to our relatives in Holland, and before this day was done, Dad wrote an airmail letter to his family in Holland.

Next came the debate about which day the funeral should happen. Was Friday too soon for notifying everyone? Was Saturday better? Mom finally decided on Saturday, May 4, 1963, as the date because more people would be able to attend on a non-workday. Having no experience with funerals, she did not know that people could easily get time off work for such occasions. Mom lived to regret her choice of Saturday to accommodate the perceived needs of others.

Now, Trudy's funeral date would forever be a dark cloud hanging over the date of their own wedding anniversary.

Visitation days were on Thursday and Friday. As I approached the funeral home along with my family a half hour before visitors would arrive, I was nervous. The last time I had come to this funeral home was three years earlier, when a classmate had died in a horrific car accident. My friend Magda had accompanied me because she lived nearby. As we walked up the steps to the front door of this same funeral home, I remembered breaking out into a fit of nervous giggles. It had taken me much effort to compose myself sufficiently to enter in a more appropriate manner. Funerals and funeral homes made me anxious, as I had no idea what to do and what to expect.

There was another reason for my trepidation today. The son of the funeral home director was my grade 13 classmate. He was a friendly fellow who had recently surprised me when he had asked me out for a date. He was a "Canadian" and I was not sure if my parents would approve, so I had declined with little hesitation. I did worry that I had turned him down rather awkwardly and I hoped I would not have to meet him here.

Today was a very, very difficult day. Soon I would see Trudy, dead. As I followed my family into the parlor, I hardly dared look. My eyes travelled to the coffin, then fleetingly, to the person in the coffin. She was wearing her pretty blue dress. Her hair was combed, but a bit frizzy. Her face was quite life-like, but different. Instead of rosy and blotchy, her complexion was smooth and pearl toned. I couldn't quite absorb that Trudy was really dead and gone from this earth.

Soon visitors started to come into the parlor, and we lined up so that they could shake our hands and express their condolences to all of us in turn. The last time we had lined up like this was at the airport in Amsterdam, eight years earlier. Our aunts and uncles had come to bid us what might well be a final farewell. Trudy had been there in the line-up that time, shaking hands with the uncles, accepting kisses from the aunts, and acknowledging their best wishes. Today was so different. I was surprised at the number of visitors. I had not expected so many. Trudy was important, important enough for all these people to come to visitation. It made me feel important.

At 4:30 pm, Dad had to go home to milk the cows. Mom was exhausted, and the others wanted to go home, too. It was decided that Corrie and I should stay behind to receive possible latecomers. Mom promised to bring us something to eat when they would all return for the 7:00 pm visitation.

A few stragglers did come yet, but after that, we were alone. Alone in the stately funeral parlor with our sister. Trudy, lifeless in the polished oak, satin-lined coffin. I was giddy with nervous energy and talked Corrie into a game. I wanted to touch Trudy, to feel what a dead body feels like. At first Corrie objected, but then she agreed and followed me. Slowly, we tiptoed towards the coffin, hesitated, then our hands shot forward and we touched Trudy on the forearm. We pulled back immediately, shrieking and running away from the coffin. Because I had barely touched her, I dared myself to do it one more time. This time, I let myself notice the cold skin. It frightened me. We quieted and composed ourselves. We talked some, but mostly we were alone with our thoughts. It was a long two hours before the others returned.

The next visitation day echoed the first. More details were arranged. Rev. Vriend helped finalize the program for the funeral. He had already found some strong young men in the church to be pallbearers. It did not occur to him to offer this honour to some of my brothers. The women's group would serve coffee and refreshments after the funeral. I drove Mom to town for groceries, and afterwards we stopped at Budd's department store to buy a dozen white handkerchiefs. "We'll need them tomorrow," she said. Kleenexes were not yet part of our repertoire.

Saturday came, the day of the funeral. I remember that none of us wore black. It was both a statement, that mourning Trudy would have been selfish since she had gone on to glory, and it was also a practical decision because we did not own any black clothing. In fact, on this day in May our clothes were particularly summery and colourful. The service was focused on hope and on the positive message of salvation. Trudy was in heaven now. She had been such a testimony in life and she was sick no longer. Why would we be sad?

As we loaded into the black limousines to begin the processional to the gravesite, five-year old Peter asked, very seriously, "Are we going to bring her to heaven now?" His innocent question made us smile and provided a little comic relief.

At the gravesite, we gathered around the newly dug hole, the coffin suspended above it. Rev. Vriend read Psalm 23 and expressed a few words of encouragement. All I could think about was the coffin with my sister in it, soon to be lowered, and then forever covered with the soil that was piled high beside the hole. I wanted to scream, to stop it from happening. There was a large crowd around us. It seemed like the whole Simcoe church as well as the Jarvis church had come to the funeral and had followed us to the cemetery. Suddenly I wished that they'd all stayed away, wished they'd left us alone in our grief, would have given us some privacy in which to bury our sister. I was brought back out of my reverie when Rev. Vriend made the sign of the cross, like Catholics do, and dropped a little soil from a vial onto the coffin. We sang "Praise God from Whom All Blessings Flow," and then, turning our backs on Trudy, walked towards the limousines that would take us back to the church for the reception. I glanced back over my shoulder, feeling apologetic for deserting her, and arguing with myself that she was not there, that she was in heaven.

During the reception afterwards, we enjoyed fellowship and support from those gathered in the hall. There was much socializing going on. While drinking coffee and eating koek, my mother commented to me that, surprisingly, we had little need for those new hankies today. She smiled with relief.

I was comforted knowing that Trudy was no longer suffering. I also cherished her last words for the little baby she had loved so much. I was told that Trudy had faded gradually that last night, drifting in and out of consciousness. During one of those conscious times, she had touched her ring, and said, "I want you to give my ring to Caroline." Trudy had few possessions, and this ring was her only piece of jewelry. She wanted her baby sister, the one she had initially objected to, to have her prized possession. I thought this gesture was a beautiful, symbolic gift for my parents.

Thinking back to that traumatic dominee's visit the previous September, and to Trudy's miraculous but short-lived remission, I was very much comforted knowing that

Trudy had been at peace about dying. God had prepared her, and He did not take her until she was ready. That was the true miracle, in my mind. This thought has stayed with me, ever since, and has given me comfort and peace.

19. GRIEF

Losing a daughter and a sister was a blow to our family's psyche. The grief was mind-searing and deep, but we did not talk much about our feelings. We took our comfort from stock phrases, that Trudy's suffering was over, that she was in heaven, and that our lives just needed to move on. Trudy had gained eternal happiness, so we were not to mourn her death.

My mother kept busy after Trudy's funeral, doing what she loved best: taking care of a young baby. Sometimes she would say that Trudy had been right, that Caroline had been sent to comfort them while they were grieving her loss.

The first weeks were hard, but we shouldered them bravely. I remember Cathy asking if she should still go ahead with her birthday party on May 16. We debated it and concluded that life should go on. Trudy's things were divided up, especially her needlework and tablecloths. I acquired two of her dresses. During my first teaching years, I enjoyed the lovely, navy-blue dress she had bought in Holland and had worn to Simon and Ina's wedding. I also kept the pinwale corduroy dress in shades of gold, brown, and olive-green which Trudy had made for herself some years earlier. It suited her colouring better than mine, so after a while I gave the dress away. I kept the removable collar as a memory of my sister.

My mother was never a packrat. "*Opgeruimt staat netjes*" (tidy is neat) was one of her favourite expressions. She disposed of Trudy's things easily, too easily, I thought. While going through a few last items sometime that fall, she picked up Trudy's diary. In it, Trudy had written about her experiences, her feelings, her longings. Mom began reading in the diary and came to the pages where Trudy had written about a certain nice young man, one she had dated a few times, and about her heart-ache when he stopped calling on her after she became ill. I was in the kitchen when Mom became absorbed in the diary, sighing deeply. She stopped abruptly, shuddered, and announced that this, too, would have to go. I objected loudly, "No, no! Please don't do that!"

"It has so many sad things in it," she replied, "it is much too personal and private. Other people should not read it!"

She walked towards the pot-bellied stove, lifted its lid, and dropped the diary onto the flaming logs. I was shocked, hurt, and upset.

I buried this pain, too. Writing my memoir has caused me to unearth this memory along with other sad memories. In the years following my sister's death, I tried to understand why my mother had so summarily disposed of the diary. Was it just too painful a reminder of Trudy's suffering? Was there too much evidence of how she as mother had failed Trudy? When she burned the diary, she implied that she was respecting Trudy's feelings. Over time, I began to recognize that my mother did not respect my feelings that day, nor the feelings or wishes of other family members who might want to read Trudy's own words, some day. As it is, the letters

Trudy wrote to us from the hospital have also never surfaced.

Soon after Trudy's death, I left home to go to Teachers' College in Hamilton. When I returned home for a long weekend later that fall, I discovered that my place at the table was gone. My mother had a very practical way of avoiding arguments about who sat where around the big kitchen table. Each family member had their own unique cutlery set which identified where they were to sit. As I was setting the table, placing my personal cutlery where I would sit, a younger sister piped up, "No, those are mine now!"

Much more disturbing, I discovered that my personal treasures had disappeared from the small bookcase in the girls' bedroom. When I also could not find my grade 12 and 13 yearbooks, books I had splurged on despite my poverty at the time, books signed by my friends and classmates, I was really upset. I confronted my mother and asked if she knew where my cherished books were. Her unapologetic answer: "If you cannot find them upstairs, they probably disappeared during fall cleaning."

MANY YEARS AFTER Trudy passed away, I found a copy of the letter which my father had written to his family in Holland on the day she died. I started reading it, but before I got to the end, I found myself becoming overwhelmed and distraught with deep emotions. I could not stop sobbing, "Why did you leave her to die alone? How could you have?" Mom and Dad had both left Trudy to get some sleep that last night while she lay dying in the hospital. The admonition of Jesus to his disciples in the Garden of Gethsemane echoed in my brain, "Why do you sleep?"

A decade later, I was blessed by a sermon on the very text in Luke 22 that had troubled me so much, the text about the disciples sleeping soundly while Jesus suffered the agony of hell. I had heard enough sermons where blame and guilt were heaped on the disciples, and I had similarly blamed my parents with the recurring thought, "Could you not stay awake those few hours?" The pastor offered an alternate interpretation, one that allowed me to finally forgive them. I recognized that, like the disciples who took care of their bodies to be ready for the trials that were still coming, my parents did what they needed to do. They didn't know how long it would be, and their decision to sleep was neither good nor bad. My parents were simply exhausted with the trauma of losing their daughter.

TO WRITE THIS memoir, I have had to reach deep into the crevices of my memory. I have become more aware of how Trudy's death affected people outside our immediate family. I have become more appreciative of how our church community and our extended family rallied around us in our time of grief.

When we'd immigrated to Canada in 1955, we had left many relatives behind. Opa, my mother's father, was still living at the time. Four of my mother's ten living siblings had already immigrated to Canada, but six siblings lived in the old country. My father was the only one in his family to immigrate and he left behind ten living siblings. Many of these sixteen families were also substantial in size. By the time I reached adulthood, my calculations tell me that in addition to our many uncles and aunts, we had 22 first cousins living in Ontario and in BC, and 100 first cousins living in The Netherlands.

We missed the Dutch relatives. We no longer had drop-in or birthday visits from Dutch uncles, aunts, and cousins. We could not reciprocate and visit them on their birthdays. We could no longer go by ferry across the big river to visit our Opa. Suddenly, our parents were the oldest people we knew, even though my father was only 45 and my mother just 41 when we arrived in Canada. In our church, the few older people were only marginally older than my parents. After a while we adapted, and our lives filled with new experiences. We stopped knowing what we were missing.

That was so for me until I attended cousin reunions in The Netherlands, which the children of my father's brothers and sisters started organizing. The first time I attended one of these reunions, in 1999, I felt very emotional. Here I was, in the midst of a large crowd of people, and they were all my cousins or married to one of my cousins! It was hard for me to absorb. My father was the 11th in his family of 13 children, so most of these cousins were older than me, and they knew me better than I had known them as a young child. They all greeted me with delightful warmth and familial recognition.

In 2002, I attended another reunion. Adrian was with me this time. I remember cousin Cora taking a strong lead in the formal program. Her father, Oom Niek, the last survivor of the previous generation, had passed away the previous year. I sat with a heart full of emotions as Cora spoke of her father and of the many family treasures she had found in the attic while sorting through his things. One item was a tape recording made at the 1963 celebration for Tante Corrie's 25 years in a nursing career. Cora had us all listen to this audiotape.

Oom Niek was the emcee for this special festivity, 39 years earlier. As I heard him speak on the audiotape, addressing Tante Corrie and all the guests present, his voice was so familiar! I was amazed that I remembered his voice from almost 50 years ago. He talked about Tante Corrie's wonderful career of service and he talked about people I knew by name. I listened with interest, but I could not take it all in. I was just so moved to be in this circle of 50 or so cousins, listening together with them to relatives no longer alive, talking on this tape. I refocused when Oom Niek said he had several announcements to make before leading in prayer. I sat bolt upright when next he said my sister Trudy's name. I heard care and concern in his voice as he proceeded to talk about Trudy's final days and her recent death. Then he thanked all the people in the room who had visited Trudy so faithfully while she lay ill all those months in the hospital in Rotterdam. This is the point at which I fell apart. I heard no more. Grabbing a Kleenex from my purse, I started sobbing, but soon I became so overwhelmed with deep and intense emotion that I had to leave the room.

I stayed in the washroom for a long, long time. When I was calmer again, I figured out what had caused my sudden explosion of emotion. It had come as a surprise and shock to me that Trudy had family in The Netherlands to love her and care for her and to bless her with visits when she was in that hospital. I might have known, because some letters were sent to Mom and Dad by these relatives in those years, but I had paid so little attention. All those years I had so little awareness of having family across the ocean. But now, I was feeling so grateful to these wonderful people for loving my sister. My tears had flowed abundantly and unexpectedly because of the shock and joy of being enveloped by a loving, caring family, a family I had lost when we immigrated. That moment, I felt immensely blessed!

PART III

20. OPENING THE FLOODGATES

Looking back at our family story, one might assume that my parents had a deep appreciation for higher education. Not so. It was not due to parental nudging that ten of their thirteen children earned a BA and seven of those had one or more additional university degrees. No, my parents were blessed with children who all found learning easy but there was no expectation or encouragement for us to stay in school any longer than necessary. Their motto for us was simply: "Work hard and always do your very best!" Perhaps their attitude was not surprising. My mother had little more than five years of elementary school education. My father had more opportunity for schooling, but at age 14 he dropped out to join his father on the family farm.

My oldest brother and oldest sister completed vocational training in The Netherlands. Simon attended Landbouw School, a four-year agricultural coop program he began at age 13. Trudy earned a Home Economics certificate at age 14. At the time we left Holland, they were both working for my parents on the boerderij. Catherine told me that she did not expect to go to high school, either, in spite of her excellent grades. In Holland, streaming of students begins in grade 7, and students in Maasland going to the high school stream took a prerequisite French class. It was offered before school during their grade 5 and 6 years. It did not occur to my parents to have Cathy (Catherine) take this class. In the summer of 1953, our family's English tutor intervened on her behalf. He convinced my parents that high school was more appropriate than a basic education for Cathy. For the next 18 months, she attended high school in the neighbouring town of Maasluis and enjoyed its more challenging program.

Then we immigrated to Canada. Because they were in their teens, the older children made the greatest sacrifices. They lost their friends and familiar culture and had little free time or opportunity to pursue their own interests. Financial survival became top priority. Simon, Trudy, and Cathy were still young (17, 15, 14) but they found an assortment of temporary jobs to help support our family. Two years later, and before completing grade 8, John dropped out of school to help my father on the farm. I was 12 at this time, and I was now the oldest family member still in school.

The following year (1958), I graduated from the small Christian school in Jarvis and attended high school in Simcoe. I remember my guidance counsellor remarking to me once that students from Jarvis Christian School all did well in high school. In her tone I heard the implication, "surprisingly" well. She was right, but I don't think that we had received great academic preparation at that new school. I think the Jarvis graduates did well because we were hard working, self-reliant immigrant children.

One day, while we were dusting and cleaning and alone in the living room, my mother addressed me with, "So, Mary, maybe it is time for you to find a job soon, to find a *'baantje op een kantoor'* (an office job)?" I was just finishing grade 10, and I had not seen this coming. I always did well at school and received positive affirmation from my teachers, who wrote comments in my report cards like, "Mary is university material."

I objected vehemently, "No, that is against the law. I am only 15, and I am not going to do something illegal like John did, quitting school at age 13." Surprisingly, she gave me no further argument.

One year later, my mother again asked me to consider leaving school and finding a paid position somewhere. I had just finished grade 11. I liked school and had absolutely no desire to enter the workforce yet. This time I argued that the way school works in Canada is that you earn a certificate after grade 10, and then you receive the big diploma after grade 12. "So, if I quit now, I have just wasted the past year. No, I want to finish grade 12." The argument was rather lame but it worked. Again, my mother backed off. I do remember hearing her mutter once that I was too sickly for work anyway, so it made sense for me to stay in school.

Inevitably, the discussion resurfaced the following year. By this time, I knew that I wanted to become a teacher. I explained to my mother that it would take only two more years of schooling for me to become a certified teacher - grade 13, which was Ontario's equivalent of university at the time, and one year of Teachers' College. She thought this was a very long time, but I appealed to issues faced by board members of the Jarvis Christian School, my father among them. The new Christian schools were having difficulty finding qualified teachers, and sometimes they hired people with no more than grade 12 education. Rather self-righteously, I told my mother that I wanted to be properly qualified and that I could help the Christian schools. My argument sounded reasonable to her, but then, after a bit more thought, she lobbed her biggest counter-argument: "What if you get married? Then you will have wasted all that education!"

Appealing to her fear of having any of her daughters become old spinsters, I rebutted with, "What if no one wants to marry me? Then I need a way to support myself." She caved in, and sighed, "*Ja, dat is true.*" I heaved a sigh of relief. My mother would not be standing in my way while I pursued my dream to become a teacher. Financing questions would be mine to solve. I chose not to linger on the implied insult, that I might fail in my "catch-a-husband" quest. I did sometimes wonder why my father was never involved in these discussions, or why there was no reference to him, as in, "I'll talk to Dad about it."

I LEFT HOME to attend Hamilton Teacher's College in Hamilton when I was 18 years old. One year later, with a teacher's certificate in hand, I took on my first teaching assignment. From 1964 to 1966, I was the grade 2/3 teacher in the Jarvis Christian School, and I was responsible for 39 students. My adult life had begun. My annual salary was $2900, and for a short time, I supported my original family with a significant portion of my earnings.

Staff, Jarvis Christian School, 1965-66: I am front row, second from left.

The family floodgates had been opened. As far as I know, no one had to beg to stay in school after that. My eight younger siblings all attended university and earned one or more degrees, in an era when such educational achievement was still uncommon, especially in rural communities. In the 1960's fewer than 10% of students in Canada continued education beyond high school.

I attribute the educational success of my siblings to their personal persistence and to the opportunities for children of families with limited financial resources to take advantage of substantial grants and student loans. My older siblings furthered their education when they had the chance. Simon earned his diesel mechanic diploma in his early twenties. John returned to school at age 19 to pursue his own educational goals, becoming a medical doctor at age 27. Catherine took some night school classes in her late teens, and in her forties, she attended adult day school, earning her high school diploma.

And me? What about me? I taught school for six years and then became a mother. I had no long-term plans. However, to help our family finances, I did some supply teaching and short-term contracts during the next 12 years. At age 37, I re-entered the workforce and I did not stop until well into retirement age. Over time, I discovered my niche in special education, administration, and consulting, and I found my work to be tremendously satisfying and rewarding. I was 72 when I finished my last, part-time contract.

In the 1970's, a BA degree had become a requirement for teachers. I took many in-class and online courses in the decades that followed, but in my late fifties I still did not have a BA degree and it rankled me. My husband had earned four degrees and my four children had all graduated from university. It was my turn. In 2004, I returned to campus to take my last seven courses for a degree in psychology from Waterloo University.

In the spring of 2005, two of my sisters warmed my heart when they attended my graduation. I was 60 years old! My thoughtful children bought me a wonderful graduation gift: my first watercolour painting course!

M. Guldemond, 2019

21. MY PARENTS' LATER YEARS

Over time, life at home became calmer for my parents. The family gradually shrunk to more manageable numbers, as shown in this mealtime photo. There are only six children at the dinner table now. One after another, the children grew up, moved out, got married at some point, and had children. My parents' family grew ever larger, as seen in the next family picture taken in a park in Simcoe.

This 1980 photo includes all of my family: Adrian, holding Wesley, is third from left in the back row, I am in front of him with baby Vanessa, middle row, and Marcel and Lawren are in front of me. My father was 70 and my mother was 67 in this photo. By the time they reached their eighties, my parents had 42 grandchildren, and the whole clan, including in-laws, numbered around 100.

Immigration brought my parents hardships but also opportunities, sadness but also joy. After Trudy died, my parents lived three more decades and these were easier years. If my parents had any regrets about immigrating, they did not let us know. Both my mother and my father focused on being *"flink,"* on gritting their teeth and putting mind over matter. Life was a matter of choices. You do what has to be done. The legacy they left us, their children, is to tough it out whatever the circumstance, and to look forward, not back at what might have been.

I am quite sure that, unlike Rosemary Sloot's mother, my parents had no final regrets. This was most evident whenever we celebrated special family occasions or when we had family gatherings at a park or in a school cafeteria in their later years. Opa and Oma Vander Kooy radiated joy when they were surrounded by 70 or more of their many children and grandchildren.

FOR MY FATHER, what was the impact of immigration? That first summer in Brantford, when he was up late at night, sitting on the veranda scratching his itchy skin? For months he was bothered by a terrible skin rash, possibly eczema, but more likely poison ivy. He said he couldn't sleep. I suspect he was also very homesick. Buying his own farm helped. My father was a brave, hard-working soul who never complained when life became so burdensome. He found structure and comfort in the busy routines of everyday life and in quoting many Bible verses, such as Psalm 27, which he had memorized so faithfully in his youth. When I found him in the Simcoe barn, singing

Dutch psalms to his cows, slightly off key but with heart and soul, was he calming his anxious heart?

After retirement in 1975, my parents lived in a new bungalow on a two-acre property near the farm. My father was ill-prepared for retirement. A deep depression set in, and for two months he was hospitalized in Pine Rest Psychiatric Hospital in Grand Rapids, Michigan. With medical treatment and intervention, he found ways to cope. He learned to bowl and he joined a league. He did some odd jobs for my brothers who had taken over the farm, and he mowed the lawn and kept chickens in his back yard.

I wonder if retirement in Holland would have been different for my father? Would he have kept more happily engaged doing familiar things? Stepped on his bicycle? Visited old friends and made birthday visits to his myriad of relatives? Would he have continued longer as a valued committee member of various organizations? Life changed in Holland, too, but would enough old structures and familiar routines have remained to help him deal more easily with the inevitable illnesses and decline of old age? Alas, we will never know.

By the time my parents moved to Hamilton in 1983, my father's health was on a downward slope. He developed TIAs and was diagnosed with Parkinson's and prostate cancer. He still wrote some poetry and some letters to his relatives in Holland, hitting the keys of his typewriter with the back of a pencil because pain and numbness in his hands made normal typing or writing too difficult. In the end, he just sat in his big, orange and brown, flowery chair. My father had become a much-diminished person. On May 21, 1992, a stroke released him from his suffering to be with the

God he had loved all his life. He was surrounded by many of his loving children.

FOR MY MOTHER, immigration seemed to have been a good thing in the end. After the first stressful and tragic decade, life in Canada gradually became easier, more manageable. Financial burdens lessened and the children grew up and launched, one after the other. When she was in her sixties, some health problems surfaced. One was diabetes, the other was a balance problem, one my mother knew to be a familial disease. In her seventies, she walked with a cane. At least six of her children, including me, have inherited the genetic mutation which we now call spinocerebellar ataxia. My mother did not let these problems slow her down. She was resilient and learned new skills, discovered new interests, and continued to tackle life with zest. Most impressive was that she obtained a driver's license at age 62, and then happily drove herself places for the next 19 years.

It was also in her sixties that a new chapter opened up in my mother's spiritual journey. She started attending meetings of a charismatic group. Dad joined her, but Mom was the driving force. At these meetings, Mom was exposed to a more personalized faith expression, one in which people talked less about what is your only comfort in life and in death, less about doctrinal issues, and more about accepting Jesus as your personal Lord and Saviour. Mom loved the expressiveness of this new faith language. Taking over from Dad at meal times, she read the Bible and prayed fervently and joyfully. In the weekly group meetings, Mom found more friendship and validation than she'd ever had. They loved her and she loved them back. She thrived on their affirmation when they told her, "Maria, you are amazing!"

This was the period in their lives when my parents were troubled by developments in the Simcoe Christian Reformed Church. While my father was on council, the elders let a pastor go because they considered his preaching too gentle, too liberal. The council also would not permit a young woman who was attending local charismatic meetings to take Communion anymore. These decisions lay heavily on my father's conscience. My parents continued to attend services on Sundays, but my father's theological foundations were shaken. He no longer felt able to serve on church council or on the Christian school board. It was a destabilizing period for him. As we understood it, retirement was the final blow leading to my father's depression.

In 1983, my parents moved to St. Elizabeth Village in Hamilton. They joined one of the Ancaster CRCs. Mom loved the positivity she found in this church and she sang their praise songs with exuberance, often lifting her hands high in worship. Mom especially enjoyed having good friends in this church community, perhaps for the first time in her life. In her last years, Mom confided in me that she was glad that they had not actually ever left the CRC church. She continued, "If the Simcoe CRC church had been as supportive, positive, and joyful as this church, we would not ever have considered leaving the reformed faith and the CRC church."

Their move to the same retirement community where Adrian and I now reside was an unexpected gift to me. At the time we lived in Ancaster, only 12 km. away. At first, I worried about the extra burden I might have to carry, supporting my aging parents and often hosting out-of-town family. Not so. Dad was quiet and non-demanding. I was just sad for him. Mom? In the beginning she needed to learn that I had a work schedule and was therefore sometimes not available. ("*Meid*, do you really go to work every day?") Mostly, she also demanded little. My mother and I had our squabbles during my teens, but in these final years I developed a close relationship with her. Their move to Hamilton turned out to be a blessing rather than a burden for me.

From snippets of conversation, I know that Mom had regrets about some of her past actions, about missed opportunities to be more loving towards her individual children. She sensed that she had not given us as much emotional support as we sometimes wanted or needed, but she did not know how to make reparations for past hurts. (Do any of us?) Mom was good at looking forward, enjoying present moments, washing windows, serving coffee to visitors, happily greeting her family, and becoming a more loving Oma.

In those last years I stopped in regularly for a coffee visit. On one of those occasions, when my father was already seriously declining, Mom sat down with her coffee and *speculaas* cookie, smiled, and said (in Dutch), "Mary, when I was a young girl, I could never, ever have imagined that my life would be so good right now."

I saw joy and gratitude in my mother's face. She was a remarkable woman. Here she was, still not burden-free after a long, hard life, going from raising many children to looking after an ailing husband, and still, she loved her life and felt richly blessed.

When she was 81, Mom became ill with intestinal lymphoma. After a brief illness, she died peacefully on July 19, 1995. Her final words for us, the day before she died: "I have such wonderful children and God has been so good to me. I cannot say enough about it!"

22. STILL WATERS

I grew up in a good home with many siblings. To raise us, our parents worked tirelessly. They loved little ones, but they sometimes pushed us out of the nest prematurely to make room for more little ones. They were always busy and had little awareness of our emotional needs. And if they did, they did not know what to do about them. Their simple, trusting life view, that God will help us look after our children, meant that children mostly had to learn life's lessons by osmosis.

Our parents were flawed and imperfect, but they were good people who did the best they could, given their circumstances. They grew up in large, God-fearing families of their own, in a deeply religious, traditional culture. During my research, I found a copy of my great grandfather's 1844 school report. The school motto on its heading was: "*deugdzaam leven, door orde, vlijt, en zedigheid*" (Oom Teun's *'Maasland anno 1840'*). Translating this to English, the school's objectives were to teach children the value of "a life of order, diligence, modesty, and virtue." Our parents certainly modelled those objectives for us!

Our parents set high standards for us and growing up in our home was not easy. Personal attention and encouragement were always in short supply. I have sometimes wondered what it would have been like if our parents had had fewer children, e.g., only four, and would have had more time to take a breath, to smell the roses, to notice us. I suspect that we, their children, might have experienced more positivity and nurturing and that we might have developed more meaningful relationships with them.

Being one of many had its benefits. We always had someone to talk to, always had playmates when we wanted them. If we needed to get away from others on occasion, we could do that, too, because the farm gave us space. We all worked hard to achieve the common goal: to earn the money needed for our family's expenses. Our group identity may have pulled us together, but there was also a strong competitive spirit among us. Less emphasis was given to individual care, to being kind and encouraging. The focus in our family was on being independent and resilient, and that, you had to do on your own!

Growing up in a large family affected all of us, for good or for ill. So did immigration affect us all! In her art, Rosemary Sloot explored the burden of the immigrant. In telling my childhood stories, I have begun to explore the impact of immigration on my family. I offered some thoughts in the previous chapter on how immigration affected my father and my mother. I will not attempt to do that for my siblings – those are their stories to tell.

That leaves one important question. Am I, the daughter of immigrants, torn between two cultures? In the beginning perhaps I was, but for most of my life, my identity has clearly been Canadian. A Canadian with deep roots in a Dutch-

Canadian subculture. I visited Holland a number of times since 1955 and each time I experienced a strong pull towards my birthplace. But Holland is not my home. Canada is the place where I developed, thrived, and contributed. Canada is where I met my husband and where together we raised our family. I love being fluent in another language, and as I am aging, I love how my first language more and more easily flows back into my conscious brain. Our family's immigration brought me challenges, but it is through facing challenges that I was able to grow. My parents made the momentous decision to move our family from a small, beautiful, low-lands country to the vast country that is Canada, filled with hills and mountains, fields and forests. I laud their courage and their pluck! As one of their children, I have been the beneficiary of their grit and determination. Because of them, I am a hyphenated Canadian.

REFLECTING ON MY childhood, I see two very distinct images. They are separated by a heavy, vertical brush stroke. The first is an abstract painting with sunny yellows, verdant greens, cool blues, and softer lines representing my relatively carefree and idyllic "Mieke years." Hints of cornflower blues and cheerful poppy reds are sprinkled in. The heavy brush stroke separating the two paintings is in charcoal gray. The second abstract depicting my "Mary years" has more somber pigments and darker tones, stronger lines and jagged strokes. The initial years after immigration were stormy ones when survival was precarious in so many ways. I was often unhappy, worried, working hard, squabbling with my siblings, stressing over exams, and frequently ill. Most distressing and painful was the loss of my dear sister. For me, the tragic story of Trudy's long illness and death is inextricably tied to our family's immigration story. In the years following her death there seemed to be less stress in the family, better adjustment to living in our adopted country. But I was no longer there. Just a few months after Trudy's funeral, I left home. I moved to Hamilton to attend Teacher's College and I was beginning to date Adrian. Trudy's passing marked the end of my childhood.

In my teenage years, I dared not hope that I would live to 75 and beyond! I could not have imagined that I would be blessed with so much to celebrate: many years, a treasured family, good friends, a satisfying career, and joy in living. I feel deep gratitude to God for giving me a long life and for giving me my exceptional, loving husband, Adrian, our precious children, Marcel, Lawren, Wesley, and Vanessa, and our very dear grandchildren!

As I reflect on my adult life, I acknowledge that there have been successes and challenges, easier times and harder times. My faith in a loving God and Creator has comforted and sustained me through the valleys and rough patches in my life. My own flawed life journey humbles me. I, too, have been an imperfect parent, spouse, sister, teacher, and friend. I have been learning to forgive others, to forgive myself, and to make peace with my past.

Over time, I have learned to appreciate my parents more and to develop stronger bonds with my many sisters and brothers. My first family has been and is a blessing to me. Many more people have crossed my path and have enriched my life. In addition to my large, extended family, there are dear friends, church friends, casual friends, colleagues, students, neighbours, and acquaintances. Each of us has a role to play for a short time in a tiny corner of this world and together we live in an intricate, beautiful, and amazingly interconnected world. For this I feel deeply indebted to God, our Creator and Sustainer.

Now, in our own sunset years, Adrian and I are again living next to water. No canals this time, just several large ponds. An occasional duck or two but no swans inhabit each pond. The Canada Geese in our village are too numerous to count and remind us that we are in Canada. Sometimes we delight in spotting a graceful blue heron. We watch it take flight, its powerful wings beating slowly but surely as it disappears towards another pond. Water is always fascinating. Sometimes we admire the still waters surrounding us. Sometimes we are captivated by the wind whipping the water into small gray waves. Water's meditative quality is most profound for me when sunlight begins to dance on its gentle ripples. Then it becomes totally mesmerizing and reminds me of God's goodness and grace.

He leads me beside still waters.
He restores my soul.

Psalm 23

My Family's Birth Order

(1980) Back row: Jack, John, Simon, Jim, Richard, Peter. Front row: Corrie, Catherine, Elizabeth, Dad, Mom, Mary, Magdalena, Caroline

1. Simon VanderKooy — March 6, 1938
2. Trudy VanderKooy — July 5, 1939 – May 1, 1963
3. Catherine VanderVeen — May 16, 1941
4. John VanderKooy — June 11, 1943
5. Mary Elizabeth Guldemond — March 8, 1945
6. Corrie (Cornelia Jacoba) Vos — Jan. 11, 1947
7. Jim (Jacobus) VanderKooy — August 23, 1948
8. Elizabeth VanderKooy Roberts — July 18, 1950
9. Jack (Jacob) VanderKooy — January 30, 1952
10. Magdalena VanderKooy — July 28, 1953
11. Richard Arthur VanderKooy. — February 6, 1956
12. Peter William VanderKooy — February 16, 1958
13. Caroline Louise Taylor — June 10, 1962

Acknowledgments

The COVID 19 pandemic deepened a growing urgency within me to tell the story of my early life and roots, while I still could. This memoir is for my dear children and my precious grandchildren. It is also for any relatives, friends, and others who might wish to read my story.

Writing my story has been a project of love with an unexpected benefit: deepening connections with my sisters and brothers. To fill gaps in my knowledge or memory and to ensure my story mostly meshed with their memories, I spent delightful hours dialoguing with many of them via phone or email. My warm thanks to every one of you.

Simon and Catherine, you were both a great source of information, especially about our years in The Netherlands. Thank you!

Magdalena, when we did our collaborative writing work a number of years ago, you helped me discover how much I enjoy the process of writing. For this memoir, you were my mainstay, always ready and available to give me insightful feedback and expert editing help. Thank you!

A heartfelt thank you goes to my friend, Barbara Carvill, for her encouragement and careful proofreading of many chapters in this book.

Sincere appreciation goes to my friend Nellie van Donkersgoed, for the creation of a professional, classy cover design.

Adrian, I cannot thank you enough for being my chief support and cheerleader all my adult years. You graciously listened to my stories, sometimes again and again. Whenever I asked, you were ready to offer a better word or phrase or another thought. You shopped and made many dinners so that I could stay at my desk, making my task easier. It might be cliché, but I truly could not have done it without you!

www.ingramcontent.com/pod-product-compliance
Lightning Source LLC
Chambersburg PA
CBHW061258110426
42742CB00012BA/1970